CHANGING COMMUNITIES

Stories of migration, displacement and solidarities

Marjorie Mayo

P

First published in Great Britain in 2017 by

Policy Press
University of Bristol
1-9 Old Park Hill
Bristol
BS2 8BB
UK
t: +44 (0)117 954 5940
pp-info@bristol.ac.uk
www.policypress.co.uk

North America office:
Policy Press
c/o The University of Chicago Press
1427 East 60th Street
Chicago, IL 60637, USA
t: +1 773 702 7700
f: +1 773-702-9756
sales@press.uchicago.edu
www.press.uchicago.edu

British Library Cataloguing in Publication Data
A catalogue record for this book is available from the British Library

Library of Congress Cataloging-in-Publication Data
A catalog record for this book has been requested

ISBN 978-1-4473-2932-9 paperback
ISBN 978-1-4473-2931-2 hardcover
ISBN 978-1-4473-2934-3 ePub
ISBN 978-1-4473-2935-0 Mobi
ISBN 978-1-4473-2933-6 epdf

Cover design by Hayes Design
Front cover image: Getty
Printed and bound in Great Britain by Clays Ltd, St Ives plc
Policy Press uses environmentally responsible print partners

To my granddaughter Rosa,

a young Londoner whose forebears

include migrants and refugees

from across the globe.

Contents

Acknowledgements

My appreciations and thanks to all those who have contributed in their varying ways, as family, friends, former colleagues, former students and community activists. Over the years you have, between you, provided – and challenged – so many ideas as well as providing such a range of information and advice. Thank you all so much.

And particular thanks to you, Ines Newman, my frankest – and most valued – critic. Very many thanks to the following, too: Ruth Appleton, Axe the Housing Act Campaign, Max Beer and Deena Dlusy-Apel, Maria Brenton and members of Co-Housing Woodside, John Cowley, Sally Daghlian, Focus E15, Jerry Flynn, Emma Gardiner, John Gaventa and colleagues at IDS, Natasha Gordon, Mohamed Aden Hassan, Sue Himmelweit, Ibrahim Isse and colleagues at SYDRC, Hannah Jones, Vaughan Jones, Elene Kaptani, Gerald Koessl, Mike Newman, Alison Rooke, the Popular Education Network, Rajesh Tandon and colleagues at PRIA, Marilyn Taylor and Chrissie Tiller.

Colleagues at Policy Press have been unfailingly supportive. Many thanks to you and to your readers for your helpful comments and suggestions. It goes without saying that any remaining errors are down to me.

ONE

Stories of migration, displacement, community resistance and solidarity

Europe's migrant crisis: Sympathy and solidarity on Kos beaches as two worlds collide

Israeli rights groups join battle to save symbol of Arab resistance to evictions: Now bulldozers are set to displace its residents yet again

We are a dying breed: two of London's last communes unite in fight against closure

Each of these stories featured as headline news in the same national newspaper (*The Guardian*), on the same day, 6 June 2015, just as I was planning to write this book. Each was a striking story, covering very different experiences of migration, displacement, resistance and solidarity. So what were their underlying causes? Were there common threads to be explored here? And what about the implications for those supporting the displaced, whether directly or less directly, as professionals, policy-makers or community activists elsewhere? How might they be working together to meet people's immediate needs, while building solidarity, within the framework of social justice agendas, for the longer term? These were the very issues that I was planning to address.

Since then, migration, displacement and dispossession have become issues of even greater concern. People are moving within and across national borders on unprecedented scales, whether displaced by violence, ethnic cleansing, famine or natural disasters, relocated as a result of (re)development projects, priced out of their homes by market forces, or moving in search of better livelihoods and security, for themselves and for their families. While there is a wealth of research on migration and its impacts (Castles and Miller, 2003; Cohen, 2006; Tunstall, 2006; Holton, 2008), there is less discussion of the interconnections with less advantaged communities' experiences of displacement and 'social cleansing' within the global cities of the North. This book sets out to address this gap, focusing on exploring the links between these varying processes of change and the ways in which they are experienced, responded to and culturally expressed by those directly involved themselves.

While taking account of the differences in people's motivations and the variations in terms of their experiences, the book aims to explore what common factors might be emerging in the current context. Neoliberal globalisation forms a central element in this framework, along with the effects of growing concerns about security, with increasing inequalities of wealth and power, within and across national boundaries (Kalra et al, 2005; Glick Schiller and Faist, 2010). There are economic and political issues as well as social issues to be explored. Unless these underlying structural factors are taken into account, inequalities, divisions and conflicts within and between communities may be being reinforced, accompanied by increasing anxieties about racism, Islamophobia and the growth of political mobilisations on the far right. These are becoming even more urgent issues in the current policy context.

The book starts from these concerns, focusing on communities' experiences of responding to common threats. Whether defined in terms of locality – as urban neighbourhoods or rural villages, for example – or in terms of people's identities and common interests, communities have been affected by processes of displacement. And communities can have an impact on these processes in their turn.

Communities can, and too often do, exacerbate the effects of *displacement*, becoming fragmented and divided, blaming each other, as well as outsiders, for their anxieties and frustrations, as a result of these processes of change (Hoggett et al, 2013). But these are so far from being the only options. While recognising the vital importance of understanding these types of negative responses, this book sets out to focus on exploring alternative approaches, identifying ways in which communities can be built and rebuilt in less socially divisive ways, demonstrating the potential for developing social solidarities within and between communities, both locally and beyond, transnationally. There are potentially important implications here for those concerned with community development, social solidarity and the promotion of social justice agendas, whether as policy-makers, professionals or as active citizens in communities, trade unions and faith-based organisations and networks.

Research- and experience-based evidence

Before introducing the rest of the book, the evidential basis for the chapters that follow needs to be outlined. There has, of course, been extensive research on migration and asylum-seeking, based on varying theoretical approaches to understanding the causes and processes involved. And there has been extensive research on development, redevelopment and urban displacement in various contexts, internationally as well as more locally. This social science research provides the framework for reflecting on community-based experiences and responses in practice.

In addition, subsequent chapters draw on research that I have undertaken, both individually and with colleagues, over many years. My own interest in these questions has a long history. Reflecting on my personal experiences, I can identify a number of potentially connected threads as these have been explored and continue to be explored in differing contexts in relation to community development and community action.

As a graduate student in the 1960s, I joined a group of volunteers engaged in an action research project concerned with the housing situation in North Kensington, West London. Jan O'Malley has written about this community-based project, which she described in terms of 'the struggles of the working class for survival in the North Kensington area, and for control over the resources and decisions which determine their living conditions, in the years between 1966 and 1974' (O'Malley, 1977, p 7). 'For many of the volunteers', she observed, 'it was their first taste of living and working politically in a working class area, of talking on the doorstep to all kinds of people and of being confronted with all kinds of problems' (O'Malley, 1977, p 44), including the problems of poor housing conditions and the threat of displacement along with the challenges of racism. These were problems that were being rediscovered at that time, as the welfare state's shortcomings were becoming increasingly evident. This was when Ken Loach's film, 'Cathy come home', made such an impact, drawing attention, for example, to the continuing problems of poverty and homelessness in the midst of affluence.

Although my own involvement was minimal, the experience also opened my eyes to the pressures that were squeezing people out of areas like North Kensington, given the profits that landlords could be making from 'gentrification' (converting privately rented properties into owner-occupied homes for those who could afford to pay far more for their housing). Challenging these forms of displacement represents a continuing theme to be explored in more recent contexts in subsequent chapters.

While recognising the achievements and value of these community action initiatives in North Kensington, Jan O'Malley herself was well aware of the potential limitations too. Community action needed to form part of wider agendas for social justice, she concluded, reflecting on the potential scope for a theory and practice that integrated community and workplace struggles. 'What remains', she argues, 'is to fuse these struggles in practice' (O'Malley, 1977, p 180). Subsequent chapters also raise some of the challenges involved in building solidarity, to tackle such forms of displacement – whether these take place as the result of market pressures or as the result of physical intimidation and actual violence, as had been happening when tenants were being winkled out of North Kensington at that time.

Following this, my first community development posting, as a volunteer in what was then Northern Nigeria, provided me with very different examples of displacement. Nigeria had only recently become independent from colonial rule, and there were visible hangovers from this colonial past, fading photographs of the Queen in local administrative offices, and a club whose membership seemed to be almost, if not exclusively, white.

As I soon came to appreciate, however, there were far more toxic legacies of empire, the fall-out from decades of British strategies to divide and rule the local populations within their imperial remit. And divide they did. In the town where I had been posted, different ethnic communities seemed to be living close by each other but relatively separately. The causes of the disturbances that led up to civil war between 1967 and 1970 were more complex than Nigeria's colonial legacy, of course. There were other factors, too, including the lethal contributions of those who played on communities' fears of 'the other', inciting people to commit acts of violence against those from different ethnic communities. There were killings on a horrifying scale, leading to mass movements of refugees, internally displaced and fleeing in fear for their lives. Reflecting on these events subsequently, the Nigerian writer Chinua Achebe estimated that a million people were displaced as a result of the conflict (Achebe, 2012).

Chimamanda Ngozi Adiche's fictional account, *Half of a yellow sun*, which is set in this period, invokes this scenario all too vividly. Drawing on extensive research, including evidence from her own family history (both her grandfathers died in the Nigerian civil war) Adiche's novel brings the facts and emotions of those who lived through this period alive, for contemporary readers (Adiche, 2007). One of the main characters, Olanna, is a young woman from the Eastern Region, visiting relatives in the Northern Region when the violence erupts. Looking for the rest of her family, Olanna is horrified to find her aunt's kiosk, or what remains of it, splintered and burning. Her uncle's mutilated body lies close by, and so does the body of her aunt. Traumatised by her subsequent escape in a train packed with wounded refugees, on reaching home, back in the Eastern Region, she collapses in a state of complete nervous exhaustion. And that was even before the horrors of the violence and the hunger that followed in the civil war. The Nigerian civil war highlighted the inadequacy of my previous understandings of racism and ethnicity. And these experiences raised questions about the very notion of 'community' itself, a concept that has so often been surrounded with a positive glow, a 'warmly persuasive word', as Raymond Williams' *Keywords* has so clearly explained (Williams, 1976). But there have been 'dark sides' to the notion of 'community' too, just as there have been dark sides to the seemingly innocuous concept of civil society more generally (Kenny et al, 2015). Civil society organisations can, of course, look inwards as well as outwards, defining themselves against the 'other' in potentially destructive ways.

The dark sides of 'community' were only too evident in the Nigerian context, communities defining themselves in ways that were exclusionary and discriminatory, fearful and potentially aggressive towards those that were being branded as the 'other'. Violence ('The Troubles') in Northern Ireland (between 1969 and the 'Good Friday' agreement in 1998 and even beyond), 'ethnic cleansing' in the Balkans and genocide in Rwanda in the early 1990s provide more recent illustrations of such dark sides. Powerful emotions seem to have been involved, including feelings of frustration, resentment, anxieties and fears for the future, emotions that continue to feature in people's responses to the 'other', and most especially so in the context of the fears associated with Islamophobia and the 'War on Terror' (Fekete, 2009; Hoggett et al, 2013; Kundnani, 2014).

Back in Britain I enrolled for further study, aiming to bring these different experiences together, theoretically, and then to reflect on the potential implications for community development and community action, in practice. As I soon found out, others were similarly engaged. British community development was being re-examined and re-invented, taking account of post-colonial legacies (Craig et al, 2008), posing critical questions about the past and its potential relevance elsewhere. Community development had been promoted to service imperial agendas, managing social change in the interests of the powerful, it was argued. But this was not the whole story. Community development had also facilitated the development of solidarity in the pursuit of colonial freedom and social justice agendas (Mayo, 2008).

Were there lessons to be drawn from colonial experiences that could be applied to the increasingly evident problems of poverty, inequality and racism in Britain's cities? From the mid to late 1960s, debates on the colonial past and the contested notion of community development began to emerge, together with debates on the potential implications for governments launching community development programmes elsewhere, to address the problems of the city in the global North. How far were programmes such as the government Community Development Programme (CDP) promoting community self-help in ways that were legitimising the inadequacies of public service provision? And how far, conversely, were they enabling groups of CDP workers to promote critical understandings of the structural causes of poverty and deprivation, identifying the scope for building alliances across neighbourhoods, between community activists and others concerned with the pursuit of social justice agendas, across ethnic divides (Craig et al, 2011)?

As Keith Popple has explained, these debates can be tracked through the history of the *Community Development Journal* at this period. Moving beyond its original remit (providing case studies and sharing learning from different international contexts from the colonial period onwards), the journal set out to develop critical dialogues, aiming to enable the voices of the poor and dispossessed to be articulated across the global North/South divide (Popple, 2006). The challenges inherent in achieving these aims and exploring these interconnections continue to the present, while taking new forms with changing contexts, over space and time.

Displacement, resistance and social solidarity pose increasingly urgent questions for research as well as more and more urgent questions for action. So this book includes references to findings that are emerging from action research that is being undertaken at the time of writing, as well as references from the past. In summary, then, the chapters that follow draw on the findings from previous research. In addition, they draw on reflections from people's experiences in practice, my own, and those of others who have been involved, as community development workers and community activists. And finally, these chapters draw on a range of cultural resources. Poems and songs can enhance our understanding of the evidence from research just as drama can illustrate some of the ways in which communities respond to changing circumstances, enabling people's voices to be heard in different ways, expressing their aims and their needs to wider audiences.

The chapters that follow

Chapter Two explores competing definitions and varying theoretical approaches to displacement within the context of varying approaches to migration more generally. It focuses on debates on transnational movements as well as processes of displacement within national borders, whether as the result of war or other forms of violence (Cohen, 2006), or as the result of market opportunities – and pressures. While there are significant differences to be explored, there are common threads with relevance for contemporary debates on the problems of displacement and dispossession in the global cities of the North. These varying types of explanation need to take account of the continuing impacts of the legacies of the past (including colonialism, colonial wars and slavery), as well as of growing inequalities and new global conflicts, compounded by the 'War on Terror' (Kalra et al, 2005; Glick Schiller and Faist, 2010; Kundnani, 2014).

Chapter Three focuses more specifically on the ways in which violence and fear of violence have resulted in displacements, with major implications for communities as a result. There are examples of communities responding in solidarity, when newcomers arrive. But conversely, such examples of community solidarity can be undermined as a result of wider policies and practices, along with wider social attitudes and fears. Having outlined the variety of community responses to displacement, Chapter Three moves on to explore ways in which communities of those who have been displaced can be supported to be mutually supportive of each other.

Chapter Four moves on to focus on the effects of development and redevelopment programmes. There has been a range of studies of community mobilisations in response to development and redevelopment projects in the past, together with a range of studies of more contemporary examples. These include illustrations of resistance to the threats to people's livelihoods as a result of major dams and mining projects in India and elsewhere, for example, as well as resistance to development projects that pose threats to the environment and sustainability more generally.

There has, in addition, been a range of studies focusing on community responses to urban redevelopment and change. This chapter includes specific examples in which residents have come together to resist urban redevelopment schemes that were jeopardising their communities, building a sense of solidarity in the process.

Chapter Five picks up on the theme of the ways in which market forces have been underlying factors, impinging on communities' experiences of displacement and dispossession. While there have been examples of community-based resistance to market pressures in the past, this chapter mainly focuses on more recent histories in Britain. It then widens out to explore ways in which market forces have had relevance in other contexts, too, 'expulsions, brutality and complexity in the global economy', according to Saskia Sassen (2014). There are common factors to be explored here, despite the contextual differences that have already been described.

While previous chapters concentrate on displacements and dispossessions in response to a range of pressures, Chapter Six focuses on the importance of taking alternative motivations into account. People do not simply respond as passive victims of the structural forces impinging on their lives. They have agency, both as individuals and as members of organisations and groups. They perceive their options and take action in varying ways, even within the underlying framework of wider structural constraints – including increasing constraints on people's freedom of movement in the current policy context.

Before coming on to consider the implications for public policy and professional practice, Chapter Seven pauses to reflect on how our understanding of the concept of 'community' might be changing. Communities have generally been identified as communities of locality – with a neighbourhood or village base – or alternatively, they have been identified in terms of people's identities, their shared interests and concerns. But how far do such definitions take account of the complexity of people's multiple identifications with different communities, including diaspora communities, in the context of rapid social change?

Chapter Eight then moves on to focus on some of the implications for the discussion of public policies that have been aiming to promote community cohesion and social solidarity (Ratcliffe and Newman, 2011; Jones, 2013). This has been, and continues to be, a contested field, to say the least. As well as exploring these debates in general, the chapter includes discussion of the importance of understanding differences *within* as well as *between* communities, if different voices, including women's voices, are to be heard (Dhaliwal and Yuval-Davis, 2014).

While these differences have key significance for the development of community cohesion and social solidarity, their consideration needs to form part of wider strategies to address the causes of increasing inequalities of wealth and power too (Ratcliffe, 2004; McGhee, 2008). The chapter concludes with some examples of promising practice, exploring local strategies for promoting social solidarity while recognising the need for wider changes.

The concluding chapter moves on to consider the implications for third sector organisations and groups, communities and social movements more widely. Previous chapters will have identified some of the ways in which people can be supported to support each other, in turn. There are potential implications here for community development and community action more generally, and for those engaged with the community arts. While recognising the magnitude of the challenges involved, this final chapter explores some of the common understandings that may be needed in order to enable communities and social movements to provide mutual support most effectively, building wider alliances as active citizens in the pursuit of social justice agendas, both locally and transnationally.

Finally, a more personal word before moving on to Chapter Two. There remains the issue of my own positionality. When I began thinking about this book, I would have described this in terms of my theoretical perspectives, bringing a Marxist feminist lens to these stories of migration, displacement, community resistance and social solidarity. But like so many of us, here in this global city of London, we have our own, more personal stories too – as the daughter of an immigrant, herself the daughter of immigrants. So I needed to think more personally too. Who exactly is the 'other' and who are the 'we'?

TWO

Explaining migration and displacement

'Humans are a migratory species. Indeed migration is as old as humanity itself', according to Massey and others (Massey et al, 2009, p 1), reminding readers how humankind spread across the globe from pre-historic times. In the past, as now, people have moved for a variety of reasons, 'to trade, to study, to travel, for family visits, to practice a skill or profession, to earn hard currency, to experience an alternative culture and way of life and for other reasons too', as Cohen has similarly pointed out (Cohen, 2006, p 8). And this includes those who have been forced to move, within and across national borders, as asylum-seekers and refugees. This chapter sets out to explore differing ways of defining these movements and explaining these processes, focusing on processes of displacement across national boundaries as well as displacement internally, within nation-states and within world cities in the global North.

Having explored different approaches to migration, including different approaches to women's migration patterns, the chapter focuses more specifically on the notions of diasporas, transnational communities and cultures as these develop across space and time. This sets the context for identifying the range of ways in which communities have defined and redefined themselves and others, within and across borders, transnationally.

Do definitions matter?

The United Nations High Commission for Refugees (UNHCR) argues for the importance of distinguishing between different forms of migration. 'With almost 60 million people forcibly displaced globally and boat crossings of the Mediterranean in the headlines almost daily', it was pointed out in August 2015, 'it is becoming increasingly common to see the terms "refugee" and "migrant" being used interchangeably in media and public discourse' (UNHCR, 2015). But 'there is a difference, and it does matter', this UNHCR Viewpoint continued. The author cited the 1951 Refugee Convention, defining refugees as being in need of protection 'owing to a well-founded fear of being persecuted for reasons of race, religion, nationality, membership of a particular social group or political opinion, is outside the country of his [sic] nationality and is unable to, or owing to such fear, is unwilling to avail himself [sic] of the protection of that country' (UNHCR, 2015).

Migrants, in contrast, were defined as those who 'choose to move not because of a direct threat of persecution or death, but mainly to improve their lives by finding work, or in some cases for education, family reunion, or other reasons' (UNHCR, 2015). Unlike refugees, who could not return safely home, 'migrants face no such impediment to return', according to this UNHCR Viewpoint, being able to receive the protection of their government, if they choose to do so. These distinctions have significant implications in terms of the legal rights of those concerned. And as this Viewpoint went on to point out, international law also has key implications in relation to the obligations of states towards those who are defined as refugees, needing to protect them rather than to return them to situations where their life and freedom would be under threat.

Nation-states have been similarly concerned to differentiate between migrants, on the one hand, and asylum-seekers and refugees, on the other. Typically refugees (those whose claims for asylum have been formally recognised) become officially characterised in positive ways – as victims in need of humanitarian protection. In contrast, the ways in which migrants have been portrayed have tended to be less sympathetic, with negative stereotyping, which has additional resonance in the current context. States were already concerned to control their borders and increase surveillance on non-citizens in the aftermath of the attack on the Twin Towers in New York on 11th September 2011 (Faist, 2006). The pressures to manage migration have been mounting in the aftermath of more recent terrorist attacks (including the attacks in Paris in 2015 and Brussels in 2016) amidst fears that terrorists may be concealing themselves within groups of migrants and refugees. Once different approaches to the study of migration and displacement are taken into consideration, however, these definitional distinctions begin to seem more problematic. Migrants do indeed move for a variety of reasons, with differing degrees of choice. And states have varying interests in managing migration, depending on a range of factors including the knowledge and skills (and the material resources) that different categories of migrants bring with them (Cohen, 2006). Wealthy newcomers, including the highly skilled transients who staff international organisations and transnational corporations, have been described as cosmopolitan 'denizens' (Cohen, 2006). Typically these have been the types of migrants who have been welcomed by governments and employers alike. Their experiences of migration stand in sharp contrast with the experiences of the most disadvantaged, illegal entrants, undocumented workers, asylum-seekers, over-stayers (those who have stayed beyond the expiry of their visas) and project-tied unskilled workers. These are the groups of migrants that Cohen has described as 'helots', a potentially vulnerable labour force, readily disciplined by the fragility of their status as non-citizens (Cohen, 2006).

Different theoretical approaches

The *Shorter Oxford dictionary* definition of 'to displace' is threefold: 'to shift from its place/to put out of its proper or usual place, remove from a position, dignity or office, or oust from its place and occupy instead.' Each of these definitions implies some potential degree of conflict and compulsion, although some people can and do also decide to move themselves from their usual places. Differing approaches to the study of migration have similarly placed varying emphases on the extent to which people decide to move themselves, or the extent to which people feel propelled into moving for a range of reasons.

There is no one theory of migration. The range of writings on migration is extensive, addressing the issues involved from varying standpoints. To attempt to do them all justice would be way beyond the scope of this particular chapter. Rather, the aim here is simply to summarise the key arguments that underpin these differing perspectives, highlighting those with particular relevance for the discussions to follow, in this and in subsequent chapters.

The age of migration (Castles et al, 2014) provides a useful starting point for examining these theories of migration and the migratory process, the concept that 'sums up the complex sets of factors and interactions which lead to migration and influence its course' and have an impact both on the migrants themselves and on their communities (Castles et al, 2014, p 27). Drawing on interdisciplinary research (with contributions from sociology, political science, history, economics, geography, demography, psychology, cultural studies and law), Castles, de Haas and Miller group migration theories into two main paradigms. Both types of approach have been contested, and both types of argument emerge in varying forms in the discussions that follow, both in this chapter and subsequently.

First, then, according to Castles and others, 'functionalist' approaches tend to view migration as a positive phenomenon, contributing to the ways in which societies function as a whole, serving the interests of most people in the process, for most of the time. For example, migrants provide labour in countries with labour and/or particular skills shortages. Meanwhile the migrants themselves send money back, as remittances, to their families and communities of origin. In this way, functionalist-type theorists argue, they provide much needed resources, potentially stimulating development back home in the process, thereby contributing to greater equality within and between societies overall. Migrants make choices, with potentially positive benefits all round. Or so this type of theoretical approach would maintain.

In contrast, theories based on what Castles and others describe as 'historical-structural' approaches emphasise 'how social, economic, cultural and political structures constrain and direct the behaviour of individuals in ways that generally do not lead to greater equilibrium, but rather reinforce such disequilibria' (Castles et al, 2014, pp 27–8). They see migration as 'providing a cheap, exploitable labour force, which mainly services the interests of the wealthy in receiving areas, causes a "brain drain" in origin areas, and therefore reinforces social and geographical inequalities' (pp 27-8). From these types of perspectives, people do make choices when they migrate, but these choices are significantly limited by underlying structural constraints.

Castles, de Haas and Miller go on to consider differing versions of migration theories within these two broad paradigms. Within functionalist types of approaches, neoliberal theory has particular relevance, given the sway that neoliberal theorists have been exercising in the contemporary context, globally as well as more locally in Britain over past decades. Neoliberal migration theory is 'based on the assumption that social forces tend towards equilibrium', with free market mechanisms functioning to allocate resources most effectively to achieve this. Like the 'functionalist' approach more generally, neoliberal theorists see social processes such as migration as leading to benefits for society at large, 'a constituent or intrinsic part of the whole development process, by which surplus labour in the rural sector supplies the workforce for the urban industrial economy' (Castles et al, 2014, p 29). This type of theory has been applied to the study of migration from rural to urban areas within countries, as well as to the study of international migration across state borders. Migrants choose to move in pursuit of better livelihoods, according to neoliberal theorists. They are viewed as rational individuals, 'economic men and women', who make cost-benefit analyses about the most effective ways to maximise their incomes, before coming to decisions about whether and where to migrate – thereby benefiting themselves and their families and communities, as well as contributing to the development process more generally.

There are parallels, here, with neoliberal socioeconomic policy perspectives more generally, based on the notion that men and women behave as rational actors, preoccupied with making individual choices in the best interests of themselves and their families. These choices are most effectively realised through market mechanisms, from this perspective, so states should intervene as little as possible, thereby enabling market mechanisms to operate as freely as possible. The impact of neoliberal policies has been to shift the balance of power between civil society, the state and the market – decisively in favour of the market. The point to mention here is simply this, that neoliberal theorists take the view that capital and labour need to be able to move freely. This should be in the interests of society at large, as the benefits of economic development should eventually trickle down. If states and international agencies seek to intervene, this should be to facilitate market-led development, rather than attempting to intervene more directly via the public sector.

As others have argued extensively in contrast, however, such neoliberal approaches fail to take account of the complexities, let alone the potential conflicts of interest, involved in people's decisions to migrate – or not. Migrants are not simply rational actors, calculating ways of maximising their incomes before making their decisions – weighing up the 'pull' factors of potentially higher incomes elsewhere and setting these up against the 'push' factors such as the lack of opportunities and the effects of violence, famine and drought back home. Nor do migrants necessarily have perfect knowledge of wage levels, living costs and employment opportunities in their areas of destination. There may, in addition, be powerful reasons why migrants who return to their original homes may be reluctant to admit that they have experienced difficulties in the process of migration. As John Berger and Jean Mohr explained in their book of images and words about the experiences of migrant workers in Europe in the 1970s, '(T)hose who have left and succeeded in the city and come back are heroes' (Berger and Mohr, 2010, p 33). Who would want to shatter such illusions?

Lawrence Osbourne's novel, *The forgiven*, provides a similar contemporary story. Diss, a young Moroccan boy who recounts the story of his adventures in Spain and France to Ismael, a younger Moroccan boy back home, is listened to with rapt attentiveness:

> Ismael [the novel continues] wanted to know if he [Diss] was telling the truth, if the story of his emigration was not a little exaggerated as such stories almost always were. The

man coming back from France was always a little Marco Polo. He could make up what he wanted. He could weave a thousand tales and no one could contradict him about any details, because those who had also been there also had a vested interest in the exaggerations. (Osbourne, 2014, p 103)

Myths about the potential benefits of migration may still abound, although the widespread availability of new information technologies, such as mobile phones with built-in cameras, may be presenting challenges to such mythologies. Migrants and refugees may still be undertaking extremely hazardous journeys, despite being only too well aware of the dangers involved, and the potential challenges to be faced at their journey's end. Decisions about migration seem far more complex than neoclassical theorists would seem to suggest, including push factors as well as potential pull factors – interacting processes and pressures for change.

People's aspirations and capability to migrate may depend on a range of factors, including age, gender, knowledge, social contacts, preferences and perceptions of the outside world. But neoliberal theories, according to Castles and others, 'generally do not consider how migrants perceive their world and relate to their kin, friends and community members' (Castles et al, 2014, p 31) or their networks, both at home and at their potential destinations, networks of information and support constituting key elements to be taken into account in the migration process:

> Other factors may include potential migrants' access, or lack of access to money, connections and information, the impact of government policies on the management of migration, the role of recruitment agencies and last, but by no means least, the legacies of historical experiences, including legacies from colonial pasts. People's choices are constrained by structural factors such as social stratification, market access, power inequalities as well as cultural repertoires affecting their preferences. (Castles et al, 2014, p 31)

Historical-structural theories focus on such structural factors and the conflicts of interest that underpin people's decisions to move. These types of explanation start from the inequalities of economic and political power within and between countries, inequalities that are being reinforced by globalisation processes. Migration provides cheap labour for capital and/or skilled labour that has been trained at the expense of others (such as migrant doctors and nurses who have been trained in their countries of origin). There are winners and losers in the process, individuals who gain but others who stand to lose out, whether individually or collectively. From this perspective migration tends to exacerbate inequalities still further, rather than levelling out differentials, whether internationally or more locally.

These types of approach have included some concern with the processes by which the less developed 'peripheral' regions of the world were being incorporated into the operations of the global market economy, controlled from the 'core' capitalist nations (Frank, 1969). World-systems theories, for example, have focused on the ways in which capitalist production has been shifting from the 'core' industrial areas of the global North to alternative sites in the global South. This has been explained as being related to technical and managerial developments in the labour process, enabling production to be moved to places where labour tended to be cheaper and more vulnerable (Wallerstein, 1974; Cohen, 2006). Jobs were being created in the periphery, as a result, but at the expense of jobs with relatively better pay and conditions in the global North. Such movements of capital were being facilitated by governments removing restrictions such as planning controls and labour regulations, in Free Trade Zones, while providing tax incentives to encourage investment. This was the case of Singapore, for example, in the 1970s (Cohen, 2006). Jobs were moving from the older industrial areas of the global North, accompanied by migrations from rural areas to the urban areas where these new jobs were being created in the global South.

However, the quality of the jobs that were being created was problematic, and the working conditions too often hazardous. As Cohen went on to point out, young women were especially vulnerable to exploitation in such situations, given the unequal nature of gender relations in these contexts, with young women being perceived as being particularly malleable, and therefore particularly suitable employees, in their employers' eyes. Despite examples to illustrate these points, such as the shift in clothing manufacturing jobs from Western Europe and North America to alternative sites such as Bangladesh, these types of argument have been criticised, in turn, for failing to take sufficient account of a range of other factors (Cohen, 2006), in particular, for failing to take sufficient account of the movement of jobs – and the pressures on people to move to fill these jobs – in the opposite direction, too, from the global South to the global North.

More recent debates within historical-structuralist approaches have been addressing these issues and criticisms, including historical-structuralist approaches that draw on Marxist political economy. They have been focusing on explaining increasing inequalities within as well as between states and regions, between the global North and the global South. And they have also been taking account of other aspects of capitalist globalisation. In particular, debates have been focusing on processes of 'financialisation', the increasingly predominant role being played by the financial sector (Lapavitsas, 2013). The nature and extent of financialisation has been, and continues to be, the subject of debate between Marxists and others. Rather than develop these arguments in further detail here, the point to emphasise, in relation to the discussion of migration, is simply this, that increasing financialisation has been associated with the growth of service sector employment, drawing migrants into world centres of financial capital such as New York and London.

World cities, global cities and women's migration patterns

These processes of globalisation and increasing financialisation have been having an impact on migration patterns in varying ways, as well as on patterns of urban development, with particularly powerful effects in a number of cities internationally. There have, of course, been cities that have had international significance in the past, world cities such as the capitals of empires. What Sassen describes as contemporary 'global cities' can be characterised more specifically, she argues, by their particular roles for international capital (Sassen, 2007). Global cities such as London, New York, Tokyo, Paris, Frankfurt, Los Angeles, Toronto, Sydney and Hong Kong provide the services that international capital needs, in particular, financial and related services.

As Sassen and others have pointed out, the service sector has been providing financially rewarding job opportunities in banking and related services, services that have been central to these processes of financialisation. This has been resulting in the movement of extremely skilled professionals such as highly educated Indians who migrate to work in information technology, for example. These typify the group of migrants that Cohen has described as the 'denizens'.

Urbanists such as Massey have similarly explored the impact of globalisation in general and the growth of the financial services sector more specifically. Cities such as London, where the financial sector has had particular global significance, provide case studies to illustrate these processes of change. These types of city have been the sites of the growth of new elites, attracting the rich and would-be global rich (Massey, 2007). Governments of varying political complexions from the 1980s onwards have been committed to ensuring that the interests of the financial sector, the 'City' of London, were being safeguarded as a result. With over 250 foreign banks and a vast array of related (and rapidly expanding) service industries (Massey, 2007), the City, in the first decade of the 21st century, was already being seen as 'the goose that laid the golden eggs', the source of national economic growth that had to be protected at all costs. (The future for London as a global financial centre may be more uncertain, however, given the potential impact of the British referendum on continuing membership of the European Union in 2016.)

In previous decades, meanwhile, the growth of highly paid employment was having major impacts in terms of increasing inequalities. In London, for example, the price of housing was increasing, along with the cost of goods and services in newly gentrifying neighbourhoods, with upmarket delis replacing local corner shops in the process. Urban development was being accompanied by increasing social polarisation as a result. Those who had security of tenure in social housing were still relatively protected, but would-be owner-occupiers and private sector tenants who could not afford high property prices were being squeezed out, outbid by those who could afford to pay correspondingly more. And state policies were compounding the problems by cutting back on the production of social housing (Massey, 2007). (Chapters Four and Five explore these issues in further detail.)

Meanwhile, in parallel, these processes of polarisation were being compounded by increasing demand for low-waged workers to fill the less skilled jobs that were being required to service expanding numbers of highly paid professionals. Many of these jobs were being taken by migrants, especially women migrants from the global South, taking up jobs in catering and cleaning, for example. And they were providing labour in health and social care services, in cities and elsewhere, in the global North (Sassen, 2007, 2014).

As others have also argued, gender has been a key factor here. Women's migration patterns have had their own dynamics, as feminists had already identified from the 1980s, when women were moving from predominantly rural areas to take up jobs in the new sweat shops of the developing world, such as in Free Trade Zones (Elson and Pearson, 1981; Mitter, 1986). Employers sought them for their supposed docility as well as for their 'nimble fingers', enabling them to undertake tasks requiring particular dexterity, as with the production of information technology-related goods. And women have also been moving to take up precarious service sector jobs – jobs that have traditionally been associated with women's employment such as childcare and domestic work along with health and social care work in the cities of the global North. In more recent times, women have also been coming to take up these types of jobs from elsewhere in Europe, from states that are members of the EU, such as Poland, for example, thereby enabling them to be legally employed and somewhat less vulnerable.

The demand for migrant women's labour has been increasing for a variety of reasons. As more and more women have been in paid employment themselves, they have had less time to care for children and other dependent relatives – a factor of growing concern, given an ageing population with increasing care needs. Meanwhile, in countries such as Britain, social services have been experiencing cut backs as a result of the policies of austerity. There have, in addition, been attempts to encourage people to purchase their own care packages for themselves. So the resulting gaps in public service provision have been stimulating demand for carers to work in the private sector as well as for carers to work for private individuals.

This has been precisely the type of employment that has been associated with low-paid and typically precarious 'women's work'. In some sectors, such as London's health and hospitality sectors, recruitment agencies have been actively recruiting potential migrants in their countries of origin, whether from elsewhere in the EU or, in the case of the National Health Service (NHS), more typically from elsewhere. Although much of the focus has been on recruitment for low-paid and relatively precarious employment, these agencies have also been recruiting for more skilled jobs.

In some ways, there have been positive outcomes. Recruitment agencies can ease the processes involved in finding work and coping with immigration requirements in the countries of destination, potentially widening the choices available to women who might have otherwise depended on entrepreneurs (potential 'traffickers') from their own communities (Batnitzky and McDowell, 2013). As a result of migrating, women have then been able to support themselves and to send remittances home, to support their families and communities of origin.

Critics have also pointed to more negative outcomes, however. Global care chains, in sectors such as social care and nursing, may also be exploitative for the women themselves. And there may be negative effects for those they leave behind, such as their own children, who may be in need of care themselves (Williams, 2010). Critics have also raised questions about the ways in which receiving countries such as Britain have been avoiding the need to invest in training staff since they have been effectively able to rely on poaching staff who have been trained at the expense of other countries elsewhere.

In summary, these migratory patterns have been described as the international division of reproductive labour (Williams, 2010). Migrant nannies and domestic cleaners have been part of a 'new world domestic order' associated with a global economy of care (Williams, 2010). Of course such migratory patterns have not been confined to the cities of the North, but they have been particularly evident in global cities such as London, with their concentrations of those who can afford to pay for such services themselves.

So, according to Sassen, the city was providing a lens through which to unpack the processes of migration within the context of globalisation more generally (Sassen, 2007). Globalisation has been associated with extreme forms of exploitation and growing inequalities within as well as between states; it has, however, also had positive potential as well as negative implications, even for those who have been most disadvantaged including women migrant workers. The global city provides 'a frontier space for a new type of engagement', in Sassen's view (Sassen, 2007, p 128), with potential for civil society-based activism, including human rights-focused activism, developing across national boundaries. As David Harvey has similarly argued, cities can be centres of political challenge, aiming to reclaim the city (Harvey, 2013). As well as being sites for capital accumulation, they may provide 'spaces for envisioning and indeed mobilising towards alternatives', 'for people not for profit', according to Brenner and colleagues (Brenner et al, 2012, pp 1-10). These debates emerge in further detail in Chapter Four and in subsequent chapters.

Competing migration theories

To summarise the discussion so far, then, historical-structuralist approaches have emphasised the conflicting interests and increasing inequalities that capitalist development processes have been exacerbating between the global North and the global South, internationally. They have focused on the structural inequalities that have been increasing between social classes, between capital and labour within as well as between nation-states. And there has been increasing emphasis on the importance of analysing the impact of other forms of discrimination and oppression too, particularly those relating to gender and ethnicity. Recent debates, including debates between Marxists, have also focused on increasing financialisation as a key factor, to be understood as part of the background to the contemporary context.

In contrast, the proponents of neoliberal globalisation have been promoting very different arguments starting from their emphasis on the importance of freeing up restrictions on market mechanisms, to enable market forces to work most effectively. Rational individuals can then make choices for their own and their families' benefit, choices that can lead to development and growth with ultimate benefits for society at large as a result. From this type of perspective, international trade and investment need to be deregulated in order to enable market mechanisms to operate freely, at international as well as at national levels, neoliberal policies that became increasingly predominant from the Reagan and Thatcher years in the 1980s.

Capital and labour should both be free to move, by implication. Except that the reality has been more complex – becoming increasingly contested over time. There have been countervailing views within the proponents of market-based approaches more generally. Even when states have wanted to enable employers to access the types of labour that they were requiring – and on the terms that they have been prepared to offer – states have also tended to hold on to the view that they should be able to control their borders. This has been a factor of increasing contestation for a number of individual states, including Britain and the US. And it has been a factor of increasing significance for members of groupings of states, as in the case of the EU, with rising concerns about mass movements of people accompanied by growing fears of terrorism – 'moral panics' on a global scale. The extent to which borders can be effectively controlled in practice has, of course, been more problematic (Cohen, 2006). Borders have been porous (Massey et al, 2009), despite attempts to construct effective barriers, including barriers of barbed wire and concrete, keeping people out. Whether these barriers are effective or not, they testify to particular politicians' interests in responding to popular anxieties. Politicians of the far right have been increasingly engaging with these concerns, fuelling the development of populist movements. While critical of neoliberal globalisation in general, populist politicians of the far right have been focusing on migration more specifically. There have been calls for increasing restrictions on newcomers, for example, even calls for the repatriation of existing immigrants, with a wall to keep them out of the US, as Donald Trump proposed in his presidential election campaign in 2016.

Meanwhile, state welfare spending has been rolled back, and public services increasingly marketised as part of the same pattern of neoliberal agendas over recent decades. State interventions have been shifted away from the provision of services directly to meet people's needs, funding being directed towards encouraging individuals to make their own choices for themselves and their families, through market mechanisms, depending on what they could afford to pay. The implications of such shifts can be traced only too clearly through the example of the housing crisis in cities such as London, where the supply of genuinely affordable social housing has been shrinking, leaving those unable to afford to house themselves at risk of being displaced, squeezed out of the inner city altogether, as Chapters Four and Five explore in further detail. Here, too, newcomers have been proving easy targets for the frustrations of local people, struggling to cope with the effects of increasing marketisation and public service cuts, frustrations that can also fuel the growth of populist movements of the far right.

Overall, then, there has been increasing polarisation, in parallel with increasing levels of social inequality. The balance of power between capital and labour has been shifting decisively in favour of the former at the expense of the latter. Neoliberal globalisation has contributed to increased insecurity, inequality and democratic deficits, according to Scholte (Scholte, 2005). Or, as Bauman has summarised the outcomes in parallel, 'The riches are global (for capital), the misery is local (for labour)' (Bauman, 1998, p 74). The results have been becoming increasingly polarised, as neoliberal globalisation has been coming under fire. There has been growing criticism from the far right as well as from the left of the political spectrum, with calls for more protectionist policies as part of populist agendas for alternative futures.

So neoliberal globalisation is being criticised from very different standpoints, as the ensuing shortcomings become increasingly evident. As subsequent chapters will be suggesting, however, neoliberal globalisation strategies still have relevance when it comes to explaining the ways in which people and communities have become displaced in recent times. This is whether migrants have been moving as a result of socioeconomic or political pressures to search for alternative livelihoods elsewhere, or whether tenants and residents have been moving as a result of government policies that have cut spending and deregulated social welfare provision, leading to drastic shortages of genuinely affordable housing in world cities in the global North (Massey, 2007; Sassen, 2007). The role of market forces emerges in more detail in subsequent chapters, together with the extent to which public policies succeed – or fail – in attempting to manage market forces in the interest of meeting social needs.

While emphasising such pressures on people to move, however, it is important to re-emphasise that migrants are not simply passively pushed and pulled, displaced by structural forces beyond their control in the context of neoliberal capitalist globalisation. They are also agents, with the ability to develop their own perspectives and to act accordingly, albeit within these structural constraints. They can and do also develop networks of support and solidarity, whether in their workplaces or their communities, spanning connections within and between their communities of origin and their destinations of migration elsewhere. Before coming on to these more collective and community-related aspects of migration, however, the processes leading to the movements of such communities need to be summarised. How have different groups of migrants maintained ties and cultural affiliations within and across national borders?

Migration, diasporas and cultural change

Cohen starts his discussion of varying types of group displacements with the case of the Jewish diaspora (Cohen, 1997). This was the case that was generally taken as the classic definition of the term 'diaspora'. From the 20th century onwards, however, the term began to be expanded to include other involuntary movements of people – with a particular focus on the ways in which people have maintained identifications and connections with their homelands, whether economically, politically or culturally, despite being displaced (Kenny, 2013). These identifications and attachments have taken differing forms, and have varied over time and between generations, as migrants and their descendants have been adjusting to their changing situations in their areas of destination. The original meaning of the term 'diaspora' comes from a combination of classical Greek words meaning to spread or disperse, generally implying that this was a destructive process, although diaspora can also have more positive implications. In the Jewish case, this diaspora developed in response to being forcibly dispersed. The first experiences of dispersal were during the exile in Babylon from 586 BC, experiences of dispersal that were then repeated following the last Jewish revolt against the Romans in 135 AD, when the Emperor Hadrian razed Jerusalem (Cohen, 1997; Kenny, 2013). Scattered in exile, Jewish communities survived as a diaspora (diasporas) across Europe, North Africa, the Middle East and beyond, developing local variations in cultural practices and norms in their differing locations, although still held together by common ties and attachments to their Jewish identity.

While the Jewish case has constituted the classic concept of 'diaspora' in the past, Cohen and others have also gone on to apply the term to other displacements of people. The slave trade provided a case in point. This involved the forcible displacement of Africans to the Americas and Caribbean on a massive scale, with appalling losses of life on the way. The number of Africans transported to the Americas during the 250 years of the slave trade has been estimated to have been up to 20 million (Marfleet, 2006). This was another example of what Cohen characterised as falling within the category of 'victim' diaspora, other instances of forcible community dispersals to be set alongside the Jewish case.

Although families and communities were fragmented in the process of transportation and their subsequent experiences of slavery, aspects of African culture survived. African music developed new forms including gospel singing and jazz, for example. Rather than remaining frozen in their original African forms, African American and African Caribbean cultures developed their own distinctive Black cultures. And these cultures have been characterised as emerging in hybrid ways, as Paul Gilroy and others have argued (Gilroy, 1993). There were, Gilroy concluded, parallels between Black and Jewish concepts of diaspora.

Cohen goes on to describe the use of indentured labour as another form of displacement 'labour diaspora' that led to the development of diasporas in the past (Cohen, 1997). Colonial powers, with the assistance of mainly British and Dutch contractors, recruited labour from India, China, Japan and Malaya, he pointed out, shipping their cargoes of technically free, but indentured, labourers to their colonies in the Caribbean, South and East Africa, South East Asia and the Pacific islands. Marfleet quotes an estimate of some 37 million people being transported in these ways by the mid-20th century (Marfleet, 2006). Although they were paid, these workers were bound to their employers through their indentures, typically working in extremely exploitative situations. Here, too, as with the slaves who had been transported from Africa, there were cases where indentured labourers managed to preserve aspects of their culture, maintaining identification with their homelands.Meanwhile, there were also examples of colonisers maintaining their own cultures and communities abroad, even if in somewhat distorted and sometimes frozen forms. The British in India provide illustrations here. On initial reading, William Dalrymple's history of 'White Mughuls' (Dalrymple, 2002) seems to be telling a very different story. His account of early British residents in India demonstrates that some, at least, of these early British residents respected Indian culture, learning local languages and, in some cases, marrying

Indian women (Dalrymple, 2002), although they did still generally maintain ties and identifications back home (with some of their mixed race children being sent to Britain to be educated/'civilised'). But as Dalrymple himself goes on to explain, this was only part of the story in the early days, before the political consolidation of the Empire from the mid–19th century.

After that, social and cultural distances became far more entrenched. By the 20th century, before Indian independence from colonial rule, Paul Scott's *The Raj quartet* (1984) tells a very different story, illustrating ways in which the colonisers had generally become far more exclusive in their Britishness, maintaining class distinctions within their own communities as well as maintaining exclusivity between themselves and the Indians. Faced with the realities of Indian independence, many returned to Britain, but others stayed on, recognising the realities of the contemporary context. Their attachments to their homeland might have been somewhat idealised – frozen in time, without taking sufficient account of processes of change – postwar Britain offering somewhat limited opportunities for maintaining colonial lifestyles (Scott, 1977). How would they cope without a bevy of servants, for example? Diasporas were created – and imagined – in varying and changing ways as a result of colonialism, just as images of the homeland were created and re-imagined, with or without reference to the changing realities of postwar Britain.

Less forced diasporas?

Cohen has also described the movements of people for trade as further types of diasporas. The cases that he explores to illustrate this designation are those of the Chinese and Lebanese traders who settled in South East Asia and parts of Africa. But does this stretch the definition of diaspora too far, perhaps? Although these traders clearly developed their own communities in their places of destination while maintaining identifications and ties with their places of origin, like the colonisers in India and elsewhere, the degrees of choice that they were able to exercise were somewhat different compared with the degrees of compulsion experienced by indentured labourers, let alone that experienced by slaves. Nor were these traders' situations comparable with those of rural migrants in colonial contexts, effectively forced to leave their homes to seek paid work in order to have money to pay the taxes that were being demanded by their colonisers.

Cohen's typology of different types of diasporas includes other cases too, including the Zionist project to enable the Jewish diaspora to build their homeland in Israel. As he went on to argue, however, there was an irony here – the migration of Jews to create the state of Israel, having led to the forcible displacement of Palestinians and the subsequent occupation of Gaza and the West Bank.

Reflecting on the term 'displacement' more generally, Jacqueline Rose also refers to the creation of the state of Israel. She introduces the Freudian notion of the concept (Rose, 2006), pointing to the way in which Freud used the term in his later work to mean 'substitution', 'something you cannot bear to think about or remember, so you think about or remember something else' (Rose, 2006, p 269). This was only a short step to the notion of 'projection', she went on to argue, so that the Palestinians became symbolic substitutes for something quite else – the 'other'. Freud was, of course, himself displaced from Vienna as an exile from the Nazi occupation, she concluded, apparently thinking that no good would come of displacing Palestinians in their turn. This theme of blaming the 'other' emerges only too regularly, as subsequent chapters in this book illustrate. As Cohen has similarly reflected, 'Migrants are always convenient targets for hate and fear' (Cohen, 2006, p 12).

Contemporary versions of forcible displacements?

The slave trade was supposed to have been ended in the 19th century, the conventional wisdom being that slavery, 'like small pox and polio – [has] been systematically eradicated country by country and is now relegated to the dustbin of history' (Koh, 2006, p 233). But this view has been fundamentally challenged, with increasing concerns about what has been called the 'new global slave trade', described by the International Labour Organization (ILO) as 'the underside of globalization' (Koh, 2006, p 234). This relates to people trafficking in its various forms, including the trafficking of domestic servants into forms of domestic bondage and the trafficking of young girls and boys for the sex trade.

There have been estimated to be some 35 million 'slaves' in the contemporary world, victims of trafficking or other forms of coercion, including child labour and domestic bondage. While the suffering that such forms of extreme exploitation cause can scarcely be exaggerated, the scale of these problems has been more questionable, depending in part on how the notion of 'modern slavery' is being defined (O'Connell Davidson, 2015). What exactly does the term mean, then? How far can 'modern slavery' be distinguished from other forms of exploitation and oppression more generally? Who is concerned to define 'modern slavery'? In which particular ways? And for what reasons?

O'Connell Davidson's study starts from the position that there may be different agendas involved here, underpinning debates on the question of modern slavery. There have been agendas based on genuine humanitarian concerns, of course, and O'Connell Davidson's approach is in no way attempting to minimise the extent or scale of the sufferings that have been the focus of such humanitarian concern. Lewis and colleagues' study of 'precarious lives' documents the extreme forms of exploitation that trafficked workers experience in contemporary Britain only too clearly, for example (Lewis et al, 2015). At some point, while in the UK, all of those they interviewed – new and refused asylum-seekers, as well as trafficked workers – 'experienced forced labour practices as defined in UK and international law' (p 2), they concluded from the evidence. And the majority had multiple experiences of such practices including being forced to work without pay or promised wages being withheld in whole or in part and/or being forced to work excessive overtime under some form of threat or penalty (Lewis et al, 2015, pp 2-3). They were in particularly precarious situations since they were fearful of being deported if their immigration status was revealed to the relevant authorities. Many were also fearful that their traffickers would punish their families back home if they stepped out of line. Such fears were making it correspondingly difficult for them to improve their situations, either individually or collectively – although the study did identify some small instances of informal connections and momentary experiences of solidarity, despite the risks involved.

As O'Connell Davidson goes on to argue, there are not only stories about people being passive victims of people smuggling, duped by unscrupulous traffickers. People do also have agency. The risks associated with people smuggling may well be known (O'Connell Davidson, 2015), but people may still decide to place themselves in the hands of people smugglers, whether from desperation, when fleeing extreme situations of violence, as in the case of so many Syrian refugees, or when fleeing extreme hardship and/or limited opportunities back home. And the more that states seek to control their borders, O'Connell Davidson argues, however, the greater the attraction of clandestine migration services to circumvent their efforts.

O'Connell Davidson goes on to point to the varying ways in which states attempt to control migration, together with the differing ways in which they define and classify different groups of people, as victims – or indeed, as potential criminals. For example, she quotes research on the sex trade, showing how, when trafficked women have been 'rescued' through police raids on brothels, they have then been at risk of being incarcerated as illegal immigrants. States have their own ways of restricting people's freedom, she argues, and their distinctive ways of classifying human movements for their own purposes.

An article explaining the reasons why Doctors of the World provide a clinic for asylum-seekers in London illustrates precisely this argument (McVeigh, 2015, p 12). As this article explains, this is because asylum-seekers often fear the many questions they face at a conventional surgery. The experiences of 'Sara' (not her real name) are quoted as a case in point. Sara was sold into domestic servitude by her stepmother after years of abuse. 'She ended up working for a Dubai family who took her with them on a forged passport when they moved to London. Shoving up the sleeves of her jumper she shows scars from where she says she was burned with an iron – an attack that led her to run away' (McVeigh, 2015, p 12). At the police station, she wasn't asked about the whereabouts of the alleged abusers, or even referred for medical treatment for her burns. On the contrary, she was asked about her immigration status and told to go to the Home Office. As she explained, 'I was very scared'. Unsurprisingly, since then, she has preferred to avoid seeking assistance from official agencies of any sort.

Women with comparable experiences may be similarly failed by public agencies and may continue to suffer extreme exploitation as a result of being trafficked, working in appalling conditions, as in the sex trade, for example. But O'Connell Davidson refers to research that has identified alternative outcomes too (Day, 2010). For example, a study of women coming into the sex trade in London found that some had managed to earn enough, within a year, to become 'managers' themselves, as well as being able to afford to send remittances back home, to their countries of origin. This illustrated the difficulties of fitting sex work migration into 'the binaries of trafficking/smuggling, slavery/freedom, victim/agent or involuntary/voluntary action', she argues (O'Connell Davidson, 2015, p 194) – or indeed, into the binary of exploiter/exploited.

According to O'Connell Davidson, the notion of 'modern slavery' needs to be unpacked, setting the processes involved in human trafficking within the context of wider structures of exploitation and increasing inequalities, internationally – too often compounded as a result of public policies and procedures. What photos of 'modern slavery' among workers in informal sectors in India and Ghana were actually illustrating, she argued, were extreme instances of much more generalised processes of exploitation, revealing particularly grotesque examples 'of contemporary capitalism's many faces' (O'Connell Davidson, 2015, p 75). So there were differing degrees of freedom and compulsion involved in the varying ways in which wage workers' labour power was being sold, just as there were varying degrees of scope for the exercise of human agency, whether individually or collectively, in the context of wider structural constraints.

Migrants and their communities

As the discussion of diasporas has already suggested, migrants can, and in many circumstances do, maintain economic, social, political and cultural ties with each other and with their homelands, whether they were dispersed from these by force, or whether they left as a matter of choice. This raises the related notion of transnationalism. Just as the concept of 'diaspora' has been contested, so has the concept of 'transnationalism', another term that was arousing increasing interest in migration studies (Vertovec, 2009). Broadly defined, the term refers to 'sustained cross-border relationships, patterns of exchange, affiliations and social formations spanning nation-states' (Vertovec, 2009, p 2). Although not typically applied to interactions between national governments, such a definition could include a wide range of interactions among non-state actors – businesses and non-governmental organisations (NGOs), for example – as well as referring to patterns of exchange, affiliations and social formations between individuals and their communities. Basch and colleagues define transnationalism in similar terms 'as the processes by which immigrants forge and sustain multi-stranded social relations that link together their societies of origin and settlement' (Basch et al, 1993, p 7).

So 'transnationalism' can be applied to include individuals and communities' engagements very widely. Migrants can be involved in the economic, political, social and cultural lives of their new communities (including involvement with other migrant communities), while continuing to maintain ties back home with their families and communities of origin. Although the evidence does not all point in the same direction, as Vertovec has concluded, 'transnational involvement itself does not impede integration, nor is there a direct correlation between social position and transnational activities' (Vertovec, 2009, p 81). On the contrary, in fact, there is some evidence to suggest that transnational identities and ties can actually assist migrants to cope and engage with other communities in their new settings. This may be due to their increasing confidence, as newcomers finding employment and settling in, with the support of others from within their own communities of origin. But experiences and outcomes vary. If migrants meet with experiences of exclusion, for example, 'this may work to discourage inclinations to engage further' (Vertovec, 2009, p 82).

As a number of studies have pointed out, transnational ties can be maintained in varying ways and with differing effects. The availability of new communications technologies, with access to cheap international telephone calls, enables migrants to stay in touch with those who have been left behind, and with those who have migrated elsewhere. But whether migrants are more or less likely to stay within their own communities as a result depends on other factors too. And one of these factors relates to the attitudes of migrants' hosts. Is there widespread acceptance of the view that migrants can engage with their new neighbours without abandoning their original identifications and ties? Or do migrants experience pressure to pass the so-called 'cricket test', the view that newcomers should support the teams of their host countries rather than those of their countries of origin, thereby symbolising the extent of their integration – at the expense of their identifications and ties – back home? These are issues that subsequent chapters consider in more detail.

Meanwhile, there have been varying impacts on migrants themselves and their communities too. The extent to which remittances promote development back home has been the subject of debate, as already suggested (Mercer et al, 2008). As Glick Schiller and Faist and others have suggested, migration can benefit the sending countries, just as it can benefit the receiving countries. But these benefits need to be understood in their wider contexts, taking account of structural inequalities within as well as between states, the legacies of colonialism, and the fears associated with the 'War on Terror' (Glick Schiller and Faist, 2010).

Rural/urban migrations within countries have illustrated these differing outcomes in the past. Reflecting on debates on development and African diasporas, for example, Mercer and colleagues identify parallels between the roles of homeland associations in both international and internal contexts. While there may be positive benefits, in both cases, they argue, the reality may be more complex. Homeland associations may indeed contribute to development, including contributions to potentially valuable projects that would be unlikely to obtain funding from mainstream development agencies. But these associations are far from being a panacea and can be divisive, potentially emphasising ethnic divisions (however these are imagined and re-imagined over time), and potentially re-enforcing the political power of particular elites in the process (Mercer et al, 2008).

There have been differing views, too, in terms of the impact on gender relations. Women are typically seen as gaining power in their communities when they migrate (see Vertovec, 2009; Kleist, 2010). Kleist's study of Somali diaspora communities in Copenhagen and London quoted Somali men who were convinced that this was the case. Denmark was described as a 'ladies' country', where men had the worst time of it. But Kleist's study also found examples of the ways in which men were trying to recover positions of power, including by creating alternative social spaces of recognition through their community associations.

In summary, global networks, such as those between diaspora communities, have social, political and cultural as well as economic dimensions. Such connections can benefit those involved, and can enable them to engage in their new contexts as well as maintaining economic, political, social and cultural links with their homelands, having homes effectively in both places. Basch and colleagues' studies of migrants to New York from the Caribbean and the Philippines provide illustrations (Basch et al, 1993). They found that these migrants had multiple and complex networks, in the US and back home, with fluid identities and cultural patterns.

Conversely, however, as Basch and colleagues' studies have also illustrated, such connections can maintain and extend the power of the powerful. Class differences could be reinforced and class positions maintained through migrants' links back home. And these types of networks could exacerbate divisions and conflicts, including racialised conflicts, within and across national contexts, transnationally (Holton, 2008).

How, then, can alternative, more positive approaches and outcomes be promoted? How can migrants be supported to engage with each other and with others, cooperatively, in mutually supportive ways? And how can communities be supported in developing strategies to address people's immediate needs while working towards wider social justice agendas for the longer term? These questions emerge in subsequent chapters, exploring the varying ways in which communities engage and re-engage with each other, mixing cultures and creativities in differing contexts over time.

THREE

Responses to being displaced by violence

Scottish gifts to Syrians: rain and dignity: Welcome
campaigns help 300 refugees adapt to new
culture and language

Police failed to protect murdered disabled refugee

(Both headlines from *The Guardian*, 22 December 2015)

As 1 million Syrian refugees reached Europe in 2015 – the biggest
surge of displaced people since the Second World War, with far greater
numbers (many times more people) displaced within the country
and its surrounding neighbours – there were accompanying stories
of humanitarian responses from welcoming communities alongside
stories of inhumanity and yet more violence. There are examples where
community solidarities and networks of mutual support have been built
and re-built between newcomers and their neighbours, within and across
national borders. But these are not the only stories. Outcomes vary,
depending at least in part on newcomers' receptions from officialdom
as well as from longer established communities, taking account of the
prevailing policy context and social attitudes more widely.

This chapter focuses specifically on displaced people's own responses,
exploring ways in which they may be supported to support each other
in solidarity. The first section summarises examples of the varying
ways in which those who have been displaced have responded in
different contexts over time. This sets the scene for more detailed
discussion of the ways in which those who have been displaced can be
effectively supported to support each other in solidarity. Conversely,
too, however, the chapter includes discussion of some of the ways in
which the development of such support systems can be undermined,
whether as the result of particular public policies, or as the result of
particular social attitudes – or both. These latter examples draw on my
own personal engagements with the community projects in question,
including collaborative research over a number of years. Subsequent
chapters return to the potential implications for policies to promote

community cohesion and social solidarity between newcomers and longer-established communities more widely.

Defining displacement as a result of violence

Before focusing on community responses to displacement as a result of violence, the term 'violence' itself needs to be defined, and this might seem straightforward enough. As the previous chapter explained, the UNHCR defines refugees as being in need of protection 'owing to a well-founded fear of being persecuted for reasons of race, religion, nationality, membership of a particular social group or political opinion' (UNHCR, 2015), outside the country of their nationality and unable or owing to such fear, unwilling to avail themselves of the protection of that country. This implies the fear of physical violence, such as the fear of being beaten up, tortured, raped or killed. But the fear of other forms of violence could be included, too, such as the fear of being imprisoned without due process.

As Cynthia Cockburn explains in the introduction to her study of peace movements, violence can be defined more widely still: 'Poverty and exclusion, as well as bullets and bombs, cause injury and death, so that oppressive conditions are with good cause sometimes termed "violence" – indirect, impersonal or institutional violence' (Cockburn, 2012, p 3). Here in Britain, for example, domestic violence has been redefined and now includes some forms of psychological violence such as excessively controlling behaviour. The narrator in John Steinbeck's classic novel *The grapes of wrath* makes a similar point. He is reflecting on mass population movements in a very different context, during the dustbowl years in the US in the 1930s. Previous ways of farming were ceasing to be viable as a result of drought, compounded by the banks' treatment of indebted farmers. 'The land company –that's the bank when it has land [as a result of calling in farmers' debts] wants tractors not families on the land', he comments. 'We could love the tractor', he continues, 'but this tractor does two things – it turns the land and turns us off the land…. There is little difference between this tractor and a tank', the narrator concludes, referring to the instances of direct physical violence that were also taking place in this context. 'The people are driven, intimidated, hurt by both'.

Subsequent chapters return to these problems of wider definitions. Just as the term 'refugee' needs further consideration, so, too, does the term 'violence'. But for now, in this particular chapter, the focus is on displacement as a result of direct forms of violence or the well-founded fears of direct forms of violence. Experiences of very direct forms of violence emerge and re-emerge throughout the following accounts, experiences that continue to shape communities' reactions and responses, through to the second generation and beyond.

British communities' own experiences of displacement as a result of violence

Britain has its own history of violent displacements, stretching from the distant past through to more recent times. To take a relatively recent example, there was civil war in Ireland before colonisation was finally ended with the establishment of the Irish Republic in 1921 – partitioned from the six counties where there was an overall Protestant majority in the north east (Northern Ireland as we know it today). The legacies of these past conflicts re-erupted with the emergence of the Civil Rights Movement in 1969, a movement that set out to challenge the structural inequalities that were being faced by the Catholic minority. There is not the space to explore the underlying causes of these conflicts in more detail here. These have so often been ascribed to religious differences – and the relative advantages and disadvantages – experienced by the different religious communities. The reality was more complex by far, it would seem. But whatever the underlying causes, the resulting violence was all too evident. Over 3,000 people died and more than ten times that number suffered injuries as the result of the violence that ensued, whether as the result of sectarian violence or state violence, including the massacre that took place in 1972 when the army shot and killed unarmed civilians on what is known as 'Bloody Sunday'.

There were major impacts on communities in Northern Ireland. Intimidation and torching forced many Catholics who had been living in predominantly Protestant areas to abandon their homes, driving them to relocate within the relative safety of predominantly Catholic areas. Estimates of those who moved between 1969 and 1972 vary between 30,000 and 60,000. But whatever the exact figure, this was displacement on a massive scale, a British version of what has come to be described as 'ethnic cleansing' in other contexts. Violence and intimidation were daily realities. As Cynthia Cockburn's study pointed out, 'From 1969 North and West Belfast became militarized zones, studded with barracks and watchtowers, boxed up in peace lines and roadblocks, encrusted with barbed wire' (Cockburn, 1998, p 56). It was only when there were ceasefires in 1994 that people realised what a distorting effect the violence had been having on their daily lives: 'People had become so used to ducking and diving' (Cockburn, 1998, p 56). Cross-communal boundaries had posed major hazards – to be crossed at your peril.

Despite these challenges, Cockburn's study did identify cases where women were succeeding in crossing these boundaries to organise together around shared interests – at least to some extent. There were common concerns, as one of the women she engaged with explained: 'We talked about our kids, employment, education, health, all those things' (quoted in Cockburn, 1998, p 73). And there were common concerns about the violence, too, including the domestic violence that was mirroring the violence of the wider scene. But the most successful example of such community responses, the Women's Support Network, was based in the city centre, on relatively neutral ground – avoiding the need to cross boundaries into the territory of the 'other'. So the Women's Support Network was one of the exceptions rather than the rule.

In parallel, the Ulster People's College was set up in 1982 to contribute to community education and development for a 'just, democratic and non-sectarian society with improved social and economic conditions and participation for those who have been disadvantaged and excluded.' It was located in a relatively neutral leafy suburb, this being seen as the most effective way to make the college accessible to both communities (see www.communityni.org/organisation/ulster-peoples-college).

Terry Robson's study of community action in this period came to similar conclusions about the challenges involved in promoting community development across the sectarian divide (Robson, 2000). There had been attempts to bring Protestant and Catholic communities together through community relations programmes (although these were complicated by the state agendas that underpinned these interventions). And there had been initiatives to organise around both social and cultural issues. For example, Dove House in the Bogside, Derry, provided Irish language tuition and other cultural activities as well as being a community resource centre, taking up issues relating to poverty and deprivation. But, as Robson himself recognised, although there were some glimmerings of hope, the possibilities of developing a common cause, across community divides, was at best uncertain.

The point to emphasise here is simply this – displacement as a result of physical violence has also affected British communities in recent times, posing major challenges for the development of community cohesion and social solidarity. Experiences of violence took extreme forms in Northern Ireland, but these are far from being the only examples. There may also be much to learn from experiences elsewhere.

Refugee communities' responses to new arrivals

There have been varying community responses to new arrivals, and this applies to those who have been displaced themselves as a result of violence in the past. There have been stories of extraordinary hospitality and generosity. And there have been other, more complex, stories too, as the following examples illustrate.

'Nobody was interested: nobody asked'

The first story comes from Montreal, Canada, with a film entitled 'Nobody was interested: nobody asked (for direct access to this film, contact deenamax@gmail.com). The initiative to make this film came from Max Beer, a retired teacher who had come to Canada himself as a young child from a displaced persons camp at the end of the Second World War. His family settled in Montreal, which had the largest, established community of Jewish migrants and refugees in Canada at that time.

Following his retirement from teaching, Max decided to engage in further study. He focused on researching memories of the Holocaust, survivors' memories that also revealed the extent of the apathy and indifference that they had encountered on their arrival in the country as refugees. Max Beer's wife, Deena Dlusy-Apel, worked with him to complete the interviews, and she narrates the film. Through family friendships in Montreal I came to meet them and so to learn about their work.

The refugees' experiences of violence that Deena and Max recorded had been (literally) unbelievably terrible. For example, one survivor explained that he and members of his family had fled following the massacre of 2,000 men, women and children in their village. They survived by foraging for potatoes, living in the woods for three years in Western Ukraine. Such stories were often met with incredulity – people either could not or simply *would not* engage with such experiences of suffering.

As the film explains, there has been a widespread myth that survivors have been unwilling or unable to talk about their experiences, finding this all too painful. This may well have been so in some or even many cases, but the reality was more complex. Max Beer found that many of the survivors that he contacted really *did* want to contribute to his oral history project. They had simply been unable to talk about their experiences of violence in the past because so many people had found it so difficult to listen to them.

This shocking apathy and indifference needs to be set within the context of widespread anti-Semitism in Canada, as elsewhere, attitudes that subsequently continue to affect community responses. The film provides illustrations of a pro-Nazi rally in Montreal, in around 1938, for example. There was outright hostility at one end of the spectrum, and widespread indifference to the plight of the Jews in Europe at the other end. This helps to explain why there was very little coverage of wartime atrocities in the media, and so little focus on the genocide subsequently, despite the horrifying evidence that emerged in its aftermath. As a survivor reflected, this anti-Semitism was "alive and well" even after the war. Survivors spoke of encountering landladies who were refusing to take Jewish tenants, for instance, and sign boards proclaiming 'No Jews allowed'. "You sort of accept it. That they hate you", a survivor reflected, after recounting such experiences. To describe the reception of these survivors, between 1947 and 1952 or so, as 'at times lukewarm' might seem something of an understatement.

As the film points out, the Jewish community in Montreal did try to respond to the needs of this new round of refugees: Efforts were made by the Canadian Jewish Agency and others to help the newcomers to become part of the Jewish community and part of Canadian society more widely. There were publicity campaigns, for instance, and there were manifestations of hospitality and welcoming. The film includes the picture of a Passover meal, organised for the newcomers, for example.

There were also examples of very practical forms of help and support. One of those interviewed recounted how J. Schreter's store, owned by a longer-established Hungarian Jew, had provided him and a group of other Hungarian Jewish refugees with items of clothing. There had also been support to enable refugees to be categorised as qualifying for work in the textile industry, with the government sponsoring a 'Tailors Project' in 1947, to bring in workers with those particular skills. One of the stories recounted in the film is that of Maurice Silcoff, a Canadian who succeeded in enabling some 600 Jews and their families to come from the displaced persons camps through this scheme, 'making tailors' out of those who had been without those skills!

Despite such positive efforts, however, there were also less positive experiences. As a Canadian from a longer settled Jewish family explained, when postwar refugee children arrived in her school, she was embarrassed to recount that "there was just no integration. We certainly didn't reach out." Others described the name-calling that went on – 'greener' (like the term 'greenhorn') was a derogatory term for newcomers. They were "sometimes treated as intruders, as outsiders…." There was "a great cleavage", "they weren't very well accepted", "they wore funny clothes", "they spoke differently". And the final comment here, "We were ashamed of them."

One of the most painful suggestions was that the survivors must have "done something" – they must have been devious, or even collaborators, since only the strongest and most conniving would have survived the Holocaust. "You must have done something. How come you survived?", refugees were asked. There would seem to be resonances here with more recent responses to refugees, with refugees being feared as potential criminals or even terrorists.

Reflecting on the reasons for such mixed receptions, one of those interviewed suggested that "a lot of people did not feel that secure here" as relatively recent refugees themselves, fearing renewed anti-Semitism. "Many of them didn't want to make waves." And some of them were experiencing feelings of guilt, for not having done more during the war. Small wonder, then, that the story of Jewish community responses to the arrival of refugees from the Holocaust was complex, affected as this was by these wider prejudices. Community responses to newcomers – even newcomers from the same community of origin – can be all too easily undermined, whether as the result of public policies, or of wider social attitudes and stereotypes – or both.

A family refugee story from Lesvos

The second story comes from Greece, 'A family refugee story from Lesvos', as told by Erene Kaptani, a community development worker and activist who was working with refugees who arrived on the island in 2015 (see www.youtube.com/watch?v=rIO_natko7o). Her account is illustrated with photographs from the past as well as from more recent times, set out in the format of a story, to engage and inform young people. Although this is recounted in semi-fictional terms, the substance of her account is firmly based on fact, as her accompanying notes explain.I came to know Erene several years ago, when she was studying youth and community work at Goldsmiths, where I was teaching. When we met up, more recently, she filled me in about the creative work that she has been doing, using community arts for research, before telling me about these particularly personal experiences back home in Greece, that summer, in 2015.

Her story starts from the arrival of her own family, 'Captain Watermelon's family' (so-called because the family had previously been watermelon farmers). They came to Lesvos from Turkey in a small boat, fleeing ethnic cleansing associated with population movements after the First World War in 1922. As Erene Kaptani explains, 'a war forced my grandmother's family to leave their homes, their beds – and their teddy bears. She [Erene's grandmother} arrived in a small and flimsy boat, absolutely crammed…. They took a great risk. They were so confused and sad as the rest of the family had got left behind, drowned or killed', despite the fact that French and British boats had been there but had not been allowed to help them.

The parallels with the more recent arrivals that Erene herself was supporting in 2015 are only too striking. In both cases those who arrived were the lucky ones, she went on to explain – others drowned on the way. And in both cases so much more could have been done to save them.

Then, in 1922, as more recently too, 'When the villagers saw them coming from Turkey in these boats they were not sure if they wanted them. They called them names like "Turkish seed", deciding that "they were not like them".' Despite all the odds and continuing pressures, however, Captain Watermelon and his family managed to get some land and so began farming on the island, building up a successful watermelon business again.

When the new arrivals started to come in numbers, in 2015, many families who had come as refugees themselves in the past welcomed the newcomers. Captain Watermelon's family befriended and provided shelter for a refugee family, for instance, delighted to discover that the newcomers had also been watermelon farmers themselves. As Erene Kaptani explained, these families came to like each other very much.

But this was not the only reaction to the newcomers. Just as in the past, sometimes people hesitated. 'They did not know what to do with the people coming in, to ignore them, to be nice, to be scared, sad or angry.'

She went on to describe the reactions of the refugees themselves, expressing their gratitude when they experienced generosity and kindness. 'They never fail to turn to us as they leave, saying "thank you" wishing the villagers "good luck" when they were moved on', she explained. But Erene Kaptani went on to question who was most in need of good luck. The new arrivals most certainly were. They were suffering hunger, sleeping outside on concrete, forced to walk miles and miles right across the island and then to join lengthy queues for days and days, in order to get the requisite documentation from the authorities.

The families of those who had arrived previously as refugees, like Captain Watermelon's family, were experiencing stresses too. They were getting poorer and poorer. They were being charged now for basic services, as a result of European-level austerity policies. And yet they were also supporting so many newcomers. As one of the previous generation of refugees wondered, 'What weight of responsibility is this on our shoulders?' Which raises the question of what support they themselves were receiving, in turn. This was problematic to say the least, given the drastic austerity measures that Greece was experiencing at that time, all of this decided by the 'European masters'.

There were further pressures, too, as a result of increasing competition for land. Some of the volunteers who were there to help out decided that they wanted to buy land next to Captain Watermelon's family land. This was in order to grow watermelons to feed the refugees. But some of the refugees also wanted access to land, in order to grow their own food for themselves. When they all met to discuss this issue of competition for land, the volunteers explained that they were offering to *give* watermelons to the refugees. But 'we are so sorry', these volunteers continued, because 'we can't do anything about the safe land that you both [newly arrived refugees and longer established refugees like Captain Watermelon's family] need.' The refugees could be given food but they could not be supported to support themselves. Meanwhile Captain Watermelon's family were also feeling insecure about their future. 'We are without a country', one of them commented, 'we just didn't have to leave yet.'

In her accompanying notes, Erene Kaptani starts by quoting a member of a local group assisting refugees. 'I am trying to bring back some sense into this madness … how have I got embroiled in all this, who am I replacing, what weight and responsibility is this on our shoulders?' Local people from Lesvos had different views about the refugee crisis. Many of them were feeling abandoned by European institutions, as they witnessed the consequences of European intervention in the Middle East, together with the consequences of European-level failures to respond to the refugee crisis effectively. 'They witness loss of life, maltreatment and absence of basic human rights, all of which occur directly and indirectly as a result of the decisions made by European institutions which do not provide them with safe passage to Europe and resettlement.'

As a result, she continued, local people 'have started to manifest signs of trauma such as increased anxiety, lack of sleep, depression and feelings of abandonment and hopelessness. All this at a time when the worst underdevelopment is taking place in their country resulting in the loss of basic social rights to access to free health, pension, insurance, welfare and housing.' In addition they were experiencing a wounded and alienating identity as Greek citizens because their affairs were being run by European committees. This 'makes them easy "prey" to nationalistic rhetoric and recruitment for right-wing parties as well as encouraging opportunists to take the lead and "represent" the local sentiment', she concluded.

The accompanying notes go on to point to the problems associated with the arrival of humanitarian NGOs. 'What about the locals? A drama staged in Lesvos where locals, humanitarians and refugees are being directed by European leaders.... Some of them [the NGOs] bring along "colonial" legacies of righteousness that are manifested by beliefs that undermine the local knowledge and ways of responding to this situation', she continued.

Meanwhile, given the pressures of austerity, compounded by the pressures associated with the refugee crisis, local people were increasingly afraid for their own futures. Would they 'have a similar fate to that of the refugees?' Would they also need to migrate to 'look for a non-precarious place to work and access social rights?... Both refugees and "locals" needed to be protected by the implementation of social and human rights', she concluded.

Community responses to refugees in Lesvos were potentially complex, just as they had been in Montreal. Here, too, they were affected by wider attitudes and anxieties. And these attitudes and anxieties were directly affected by public policies and practices in turn. So how might community development contribute to supporting communities to address these challenges?

Praxis Community Projects: supporting people to develop communities of support

Praxis is a community development organisation based in the East End of London. As their website explains,

> Praxis Community Projects is committed to working with vulnerable migrants. We are deeply concerned for the safety and wellbeing of refugees, asylum seekers, refused asylum seekers, people with limited or no recourse to public funds as a result of their migration status, young unaccompanied asylum seekers, victims of human trafficking, foreign national offenders and others who find it difficult to settle in the UK. (www.praxis.org.uk/)

When my colleagues were working in partnership with Praxis to explore the most effective ways of evaluating their impact on people's lives and communities, the organisation was providing 'advice, training, group work and interpreting to over 14,000 people each year' (Jones et al, 2013, p 45). Through its casework and projects it was addressing 'urgent issues of discrimination and exploitation in the area of immigration law; homelessness and poor housing, unemployment, underemployment and exploitation in the workplace, access to health care, and maintaining and building social and family life' (Jones et al, 2013, p 45). As its name suggests, Praxis has 'the concept of learning through doing and reflecting on action, at its heart.' For some 30 years, the project has been both providing services to individuals and community development support, working with communities to support them to support each other. There have been very valuable practice learning opportunities at Praxis as a result, opportunities that have been appreciated by a number of the students that I supervised on practice placements over the years.

Praxis's origins go back to the 1980s. Inspired by the approaches that were being developed by Paulo Freire and other liberation theologians from the global South, Christian Socialists set out to apply these to the problems of poverty and racism in contemporary Britain. Initially based in the central West End district of London, the then director, Vaughan Jones, began to bring together groups of those with similar interests, including those from Latin American and Southern African backgrounds. These groups included refugees from the military coup in Chile in 1973 and from apartheid Namibia and South Africa. Rather than being passive recipients of services – or voiceless foot soldiers in other movements – many of these refugees wanted to self-organise as communities themselves. This was the background for Praxis' commitment to supporting community development alongside service delivery, right from the start.

As the project developed there were discussions about whether a less socially advantaged area might be a better location for Praxis. So a potentially suitable church was identified in Bethnal Green, East London. This church turned out to have its own history as a meeting place for earlier generations of refugees, the Huguenots, who had fled from religious persecution in France in the 17th century. This had been a locally engaged church in the past, but the neighbouring housing estate, where many of the active members of its congregation had been living, had been sold off by the local authority. As a result, the bulk of the congregation had been decanted from the area, moved on ('socially cleansed') elsewhere.

Dispersal turned out to have been a common theme in the area, in fact. Despite the processes of decanting, a small community of old 'East Enders' remained, people who had had their own experiences of dispersal during the Second World War and the Blitz. Praxis organised group discussions of people with these experiences of displacement as the result of war and violence, experiences that chimed with those of so many of the refugees. Was there something in the DNA of the place, Vaughan Jones wondered, 'bridging distinctions between first and third world, refugees and local communities?'

Meanwhile, by the 1990s, there were changes among refugee populations in London. Many Namibians were able to return home (some of them in a plane specially chartered by the UNHCR for the purpose) along with some South Africans, with the end of the apartheid regime. And newcomers were arriving, including Latin Americans, Somalis (fleeing the civil war there), and refugees from other African countries including Rwandans following the genocide in 1994.

Given these backgrounds of violent conflict, there were, unsurprisingly, differences within these communities as well as between longer-established groups and the newer arrivals more generally. This posed particular challenges for Praxis. It was very difficult to assess who had been a perpetrator of genocidal violence and who was actually a victim. Praxis focused on community needs as well as individual needs, regardless of people's formal immigration status as refugees or not.

Despite funding challenges, following the 2008 financial crisis Praxis continued to be committed to balancing the need to provide support to individuals with the need to maintain their role in terms of advocacy and of building a countervailing culture, rooted in the founding values (Vaughan Jones also recognised that although the essence was still alive, liberation theology had, itself, been under mounting attack since the 1980s, more generally, including pressure from Pentecostal movements, with backing from the US).

Since Vaughan Jones' retirement, his successor had been taking Praxis' work forward, addressing the challenges of these continuing pressures. For example, Praxis used to undertake a considerable amount of legal work, but restrictions on the availability of funding via legal aid had made this kind of work increasingly problematic. Praxis had some 600 immigration cases on the books, still, at the time of these discussions in 2015, but most had no access to legal aid funds. There are resonances here with the findings from other studies (including research that I had been directly involved in) concerning the impact of these relatively recent public policy changes, undermining access to justice for disadvantaged communities, including migrants and refugees (Mayo et al, 2014; Mayo and Koessl, 2015).

Praxis had also been affected by the increasing use of contracting procedures that tend to result in large providers (such as SERCO and

G4S) being disproportionately likely to win contracts. Where such large contractors involved smaller providers, such as Praxis, this tended to be as 'bid candy', but with the risks passed disproportionally on to the smaller providers once the contract had been obtained. This resonates with findings from other research studies on the impact of these pressures on the voluntary and community sector more widely (Milbourne, 2013; Kenny et al, 2015).

Faced with these challenges, the key priority for Praxis had been to ensure that vulnerable migrants were receiving the advice and support that they needed. This involved providing services directly to the individuals concerned *and* working with other third sector organisations to enable them to respond to these needs themselves. Together, third sector organisations could also respond, challenging some of the myths that were being spread about migration in general and migrants more specifically. And together, they could collaborate to ensure that migrants' own voices could be heard. This approach also involved group work to facilitate peer-to-peer support, enabling self-advocacy to be undertaken.

Reflecting on Praxis' continuing commitment to working with communities as well as with individuals, Vaughan Jones posed new questions about the nature of community itself. This was not only about neighbourhood and the nature of 'neighbourhood'. Migrant communities such as the Chilean community, for example, had been providing support networks for each other that went way beyond any neighbourhood base. 'People look after each other', Vaughan Jones explained. But people's concepts of community and solidarity were not necessarily based on shared neighbourhoods in Britain. Migrants were also, in many cases, identifying with diaspora communities and transnational communities. Praxis itself had become super diverse, he added. 'People can and do come together around shared interests that do not necessarily correspond to geography or to ethnic identity.'

The contribution of community arts work was centrally important here, in his view. 'Saying who you are through your arts and culture enables people to assert their humanity when this has been under attack', he explained, 'so much happens in the group.' The arts work had been 'really transformative.'

I was able to observe this for myself when I had the opportunity to participate in one of Praxis's projects, the Family Support Group, over a number of weeks in the autumn of 2015. The Family Support Group was meeting at Praxis, on a weekly basis, supported by Emma Gardiner, the community development worker who facilitated the group. There were women from Africa, Asia and Latin America (along with some of their children), women from widely differing backgrounds. Although they had varying immigration statuses (the details of who had precisely what status was confidential), it seemed clear that many, if not all of them, had only too vivid memories of violence of one form or another – violence was their common background. The following account describes the first session that I attended.

As a dozen or so women came in to the session, they chatted among each other, swapping information and advice about some of the practical issues that were being encountered. These included discussion of the costs of housing/rent in different areas (how to look for more genuinely affordable accommodation), opportunities for identifying resources for student support, and job opportunities (sharing information about where temporary work was becoming available in West End shops, in the run-up to Christmas, for example). Photos of a family wedding were also shared. This was the context for the rest of the afternoon – warm and mutually supportive, friendly and good humoured.

The session was focused on planning a short dramatic presentation for the event that Praxis was organising to mark Human Rights Day on 10 December 2015. Discussions on this began with an invitation for each person to identify one aspect of their experience as a group that they had been particularly proud of and/or particularly enjoyed over the past period. For example, this might include the poem that they had prepared together and read, each taking a turn, for International Women's Day celebrations, earlier in the year. The poem was quoted a number of times along with some of the group's other activities over the past few months:

"The poem – this was amazing – and the dancing", as one of them commented, for example. "We are coming here [because] we enjoy, we do exercise, dancing, singing for International Women's Day", added another. And these activities were evidently linked to the ways in which the group was providing mutual support, in this safe space. "When we come together this place is where we share our feelings", one of them explained. "We go through hardships but when we share we are supporting each other always." "This place is where people smile … we were feeling lonely – here we are a family – there is a peace when you enter here", added another.

> 'People [here] give you hope. Before you lost everything. We don't want to go back. We want to go forward…. Outside there is tough. This place you are free – you put horrible things outside. No more pain.'

The next exercise was to brainstorm words that best described the Family Support Group and to write these words on flipchart paper. Here are examples of some of the words I recorded at the time:

- Safe place
- Laughter
- Creativity
- Human rights ("Before I didn't know my rights – we learn about your rights")
- Empowerment (through knowing human rights).

There were also a number of fuller comments and reflections, highlighting the ways in which group members were supporting each other, dealing with very practical problems as well as enabling each other to cope with the effects of past violence and present feelings of loss. "Coming here I learned how to go out [including finding one's way and coping with the public transport system]", as one explained. "Before I didn't have any confidence. I cried a lot", another added. "I lost my children for 10 years. It was too hard for me…. I cry for them less because of the group support. I feel like I have a family. I cry less now", confirmed a third.

After this brainstorm there was a brief break for tea, coffee and healthy snacks (evidently much appreciated).

The next activity was a warm-up exercise (led by one of the group). The group then split into two work groups to prepare human statues representing words that had been written on the flip chart sheets, for example, 'support'. Each group presented three statues to the other group, stimulating discussion as to how they might be further improved to convey their messages more effectively. These statues would form the basis of discussions, planning the drama to be performed for the Human Rights Day event on 10 December 2015.

Finally, one of the group members led a round-up 'check-in' discussion. Each member had the space to 'check in', to share how they had been feeling over the past week, receiving support, advice and encouragement from the others where needed. In a couple of cases, more specific advice from Praxis staff was also made available at the end of the session.

Overall, this final session provided powerful evidence in support of the positive comments that the participants had made earlier, illustrating precisely how the group provided such a supportive, encouraging, safe and peaceful environment.

Subsequent sessions followed a similar pattern, although there were some differences in terms of those who were able to attend, for a variety of reasons. In the next 'check-in' discussion several women referred to health issues, their own and those of friends, for instance, illustrating the types of issues that were affecting their attendance. Despite such underlying problems, however, the atmosphere was as good humoured as on the previous occasion. Rehearsals for the Human Rights Day event focused on the five examples of power that had been chosen – with much laughter as various approaches were explored.

The final performance, on Human Rights Day, was a triumph of energy and enthusiasm. If not the smoothest performance ever, it was certainly well appreciated by the audience, and evidently much enjoyed by the women themselves (and by their children, one very small child insisting on joining in the action, on stage).I was subsequently reminded that this particular group had been meeting over a considerable period of time. Many of the women had been attending for a year or more. This was an important point to bear in mind. Relationships of trust take time to develop but are essential if people are to build networks of mutual support. This would seem to be especially relevant when people have been the victims of traumatic and potentially undermining experiences in the past.

Community development and Somali youth

There are similarities as well as differences between people's experiences of engagement with community development support at Praxis, and Somali young people's experiences of self-organising, in London, over a comparable period of time. Both sets of experiences demonstrate the value of support, to facilitate self-organisation and solidarity. But both have been, to a greater or lesser extent, affected by the wider policy context and by wider political attitudes and events.

Like many of those involved at Praxis, some young Somali people came to the UK directly as refugees from violence. But others had been born in London or elsewhere in other countries on the way, as the children of refugees who were travelling on from one country to another, in search of safety from the violence back home. Their experiences of violence might have been less direct, but this is in no way to minimise the impact of experiences of violence and loss on the next generation.

Somali communities have had their own traditions of mutual support, with international networks across Africa, the Middle East, Europe and North America (Horst, 2006), despite significant differences within and between communities, including differences arising from Somalia's past experiences under various colonial powers, as well as relating to clan and kinship loyalties.

Differences such as those between clans could be perceived negatively, but they could provide vital sources of support and mutual aid. Remittances have been central to these transnational networks and ties, with families back in Somaliland, and the Dadaab refugee camp where some 350,000 people have been located across the Kenyan border, dependent on these remittances for their very survival. Thousands of pounds have been sent, often over a number of years, as those who have left have responded to the requests of those in need back home as well as the needs of those in refugee camps. Lindley's study of Somali communities in Hargeisa, Somaliland, Eastleigh, Nairobi, Kenya and London is entitled *The early morning call* (Lindley, 2010), referring to the long distance telephone calls through which these requests have tended to be made (made early in the morning to try to ensure that the potential donor would still be at home, and so unable to evade the caller's request).

These remittances have been described as 'the backbone of the Somaliland economy'. They have been seen as contributing to the development of businesses there, as well as contributing to families' survival more generally. So there have been benefits overall, to communities as well as to individuals and families, promoting development – even if the scale of remittances has rarely been sufficient to 'significantly erode wider structural constraints', in Lindley's view (2010, p 147).

But there have also been more problematic aspects. Pressures to send remittances may have involved sacrifices for some of those who were struggling to survive themselves, abroad, while maintaining their financial commitments elsewhere. 'They think I never give them enough', as one of those in Lindley's study explained (quoted in Lindley, 2010, p 136). Remittances may also have been used, in some cases, to buy weapons during the civil war, it has been suggested (Lindley, 2010). More recently, in the context of the 'War on Terror', remittances have been perceived more negatively still, resulting in the imposition of banking controls, with popular perceptions that remittances have been linked to the provision of resources for terrorism, amplifying fears of Somali people as potentially, if not actually, dangerous.

Like so many migrant and refugee communities, the Somali community has had to contend with their share of negative stereotyping. Lindley's study refers to Somali diaspora communities being seen as 'wasters and warmongers', although she did also find examples of more positive attitudes, with some recognition of Somali exiles as educated and peaceful people (Lindley, 2010, p 145). Horst's study identified similarly pejorative views. She quite explicitly set out to challenge such stereotypes, showing Somali refugees as 'neither vulnerable victims' without agency to support each other, nor as 'cunning crooks' (Horst, 2006, p 2) – stereotypes of refugees and asylum-seekers with all too contemporary resonance more generally. Rather, Horst herself viewed the Somali refugees she studied in Kenya as *human beings* trying to deal with the *inhuman* aspects of their past and present experiences.

Whether in refugee camps in a neighbouring country or elsewhere, Somali communities have had strong traditions of self-help, mutual support and transnational solidarity. These traditions could be supported and enhanced by public policies and voluntary and community efforts. But conversely, they could be undermined, and Somali communities subjected to discrimination and prejudice, linked to wider attitudes and political fears. Both of these possibilities have applied to the experiences of young Somali people in London.

The Somali Youth Development Resource Centre (SYDRC) in Kentish Town, North London, is another example of an organisation that I have had the privilege of working with over a number of years. As in the case of Praxis, SYDRC has hosted very successful student placements. There have also been linked research projects, and a PhD study entitled 'Transnational active citizens: Theorizing the experiences of young Somali males in London', successfully completed by one of SYDRC's active members, Mohamed Aden Hassan.

SYDRC works with and for young Somali people, managed by young Somali people themselves in that part of North London and neighbouring boroughs. The organisation has been successful in obtaining back-up resources to address the key issues facing young Somali people, including gang-related activities, knife and gun crime, educational under-achievement, school exclusions and anti-social behaviour (problems that have been facing young people more generally too, of course).

The organisation was set up in 2000, the immediate trigger being concerns about educational under-achievement among Somali young people, who were disproportionately at risk of leaving school with few or no formal qualifications. Research commissioned by the local authority (from London University's Institute of Education) was indicating that on average, only 3.1% of pupils of Somali origin were obtaining the target of five grade A*-C level passes at GCSE level compared with the local average of 47% of pupils achieving this level in the borough. So SYDRC set out to tackle the problem. Through consistent efforts with parents and schools, as well as through their work with the young people themselves, SYDRC succeeded in contributing to a major turnaround. Each year these significant achievements were marked with an awards ceremony attended by those concerned, including local councillors and others from the local community, as well as the young people who were being congratulated on their attainments and their families.

Until 2013 that was, after which the situation began to deteriorate. Educational achievements began to drop off, while the number of school exclusions began to rise – with young people of Somali origin disproportionately at risk compared with the local authority average. SYDRC has responded in collaboration with the local authority and volunteer researchers to explore the reasons for this, as the first step towards developing a strategy to address these problems. Were the problems concentrated in specific schools, and if so, were there particular reasons for this? The Communities Empowerment Network produced national research, recording parents' anxieties that school exclusions were being applied in discriminatory ways, leaving the most vulnerable young people, including young Black people, at greater risk of being excluded rather than being supported and rehabilitated. Might these concerns apply to Somali young people? Could the fact that resources for home school liaison workers had been reduced, as the result of budget constraints, have relevance? Were public policy changes having an impact on local authorities' abilities to address such issues strategically? And most disturbingly, were young Somali people becoming increasingly disaffected and alienated, in the context of Islamophobia and the War on Terror? These were among the questions to be explored, as Chapter Eight explains in the context of policy discussions more generally.

Meanwhile, in addition to its focus on educational achievement, SYDRC had also been developing wider initiatives to enable the voices of young Somali people to be heard more effectively. Concerns had been raised by a number of government departments and by the police, focusing on the lack of integration and self-representation of the Somali community in mainstream UK society. In response, supported by SYDRC, the London Somali Youth Forum (LSYF) was established in 2008. I had the opportunity to attend an early meeting at City Hall, the headquarters of the Greater London Authority (GLA), an event that brought groups of highly articulate young Somali people together in dialogue with a range of policy-makers and service providers. As Mohamed Aden Hassan's thesis points out, this initiative was widely appreciated, LSYF being awarded the prestigious Community Engaging

Award at the London Week of Peace in 2009, accompanied by press comments on the ways in which Somali people in Britain were finding their voice at last (Hassan, 2013). The GLA adopted the LSYF model of ambassadorship as the most effective way to represent the integration of children and young migrants in London as part of the fourth Integrating Cities conference held in London the following year.

So this initiative had seemed significant in terms of youth and community work. Young Somali people were self-organising, and were making their voices heard more effectively, as active citizens. Or were they? Whatever their successes in terms of self-organising in London, young Somali people were also facing challenges. They were affected as a result of shrinking resources in a period of austerity more generally. And most significantly, they were facing challenges that related to wider political attitudes and events. As with the practice of sending remittances, it emerged, some of the most potentially problematic challenges related to Somali young people's transnational interests and ties, such ties being widely viewed with suspicion and fear.

From their inception, SYDRC and LSYF had been explicitly concerned to counteract such concerns. The values set out on SYDRC's website emphasise 'Respect for the principles of tolerance, honesty, integrity, trust and decency' (see www.sydrc.org). The youth conference that was organised in 2008 included active participation from the Metropolitan Police, as well as from a range of other official agencies. So far, so good. But these were potentially sensitive relationships to develop in the context of the War on Terror and public policies to fight against radicalisation.

As Mohamed Aden Hassan's research demonstrated, young Somali males were growing up against a background of negative stereotyping – depicted as 'un-British', or worse, as violent and aggressive with little regard for the law (referring to headlines in *The Sun* newspaper on 'How Muslims took over the British underworld', for example; see Sullivan, 2009). The young people who were interviewed for Mohamed Aden Hassan's study had a range of responses to such attitudes and anxieties, with varied effects, in terms of their perceptions of themselves and their place in British society.

In particular there were concerns that UK security forces were harassing young Somali people as part of attempts to recruit them as informers (Verkaik, 2009). Such anxieties had an impact on relationships of trust, putting pressure on those who were prepared to respond to invitations to consult with the forces of law and order. Tactless approaches could undermine potentially fragile relationships of trust, leaving those who responded to such consultations open to suspicion from their peers. Were they actually informing against their own communities? Mohamed Aden Hassan quotes police questions such as the following, for illustration:

> Do you feel that there are Somalis within your community who want to attack the UK? Are you aware of people within the community being radicalised, or people attempting to radicalise others? Are you aware of anyone wanting, or planning to go and fight in Somalia? (Hassan, 2013, p 224)

Conversely, however, those who declined to participate in such discussions, or to respond to such questions, could feel at risk of being labelled as potential terrorists themselves.

There are parallels here with the findings of Hannah Jones' study, exploring understandings of community cohesion policies as these were being translated into practice (Jones, 2013). Here, too, there was evidence that interventions to prevent violent extremism, including ill-considered questioning, could backfire, as Chapter Eight explores later, in further detail. The title of one of her chapters provides a caricature of such questioning, 'Is there anything the council did that distracted you from extremism?' (Jones, 2013).

Governments have tended to deny that there has been any connection between British foreign policy interventions on the one hand, and processes of radicalisation among young British Muslims on the other. But others have expressed very different views. British foreign policy has been having a profoundly negative impact, along with state surveillance policies set against the background of increasing Islamophobia more widely (Fekete, 2009; Kundnani, 2014).

Young Somali people who featured in Mohamed Aden Hassan's study certainly expressed such views. As one of the outreach workers explained, "The outreach workers will try to make sure these young people do not get involved in activities that are seen as radicalising." But "young people are able to think. They are not idiots", he continued. And "foreign policy does make a huge impact in [what] young people think" (referring to bombings in Libya at that time, despite it being a UN no-fly zone). "Actually the government blames mosques and other areas [where] young people are being radicalised, but I would say that the government radicalised the young people with the foreign policy." He went on to cite Somalia's own problems, including the civil war, as resulting from international intervention (Hassan, 2013, p 226). Similar views were fairly widespread among the young people themselves. For example, they spoke of feeling targeted at airport security for no apparent reason, that they had become citizen suspects, 'the victims of ongoing, structural prejudice' (Clifford, 1997, p 251) – although these were by no means the only views.

None of this is to suggest that there have not been serious issues to address. International terrorism has been of increasing concern, in Britain, as elsewhere, and particularly so in the wake of the London bombings of 2007 and subsequent attacks elsewhere, including the attacks that were perpetrated in Paris in 2015. The point is absolutely not to underestimate the seriousness of terrorist threats but simply to emphasise the importance of addressing the causes of these challenges, working with communities in ways that support their own efforts, rather than increasing the levels of alienation and disaffection, especially among the young.

These issues emerged particularly clearly in Mohamed Aden Hassan's account of his trip, accompanying a group of young Somali males from West London, going to Somaliland for a football tournament. This was the first trip of its kind to be organised by a voluntary organisation (West London Somaliland Community). Somaliland had declared independence from the rest of Somalia, after the collapse of the Somali state in the early 1990s, and was relatively more peaceful. So this meant that it was possible to organise a visit. The trip was supported by the Somaliland government that assisted with logistics and transport, as well as organising a number of welcome receptions.

This all made great impressions on the young Londoners. They expressed increased appreciation of the relative advantages that they had back in London, such as access to free education and healthcare, and access to clean water, advantages that they had previously taken for granted. As one of them explained, he had been impressed with the contrasts in Somaliland. 'We came to matches with full kits and track suits, and they [that is, the Somaliland teams] with not even shin pads.' He went on to add that he had arrived wearing headphones, not having appreciated that headphones were a luxury that others could not possibly afford. Having realised that 'I have it good in London' (relatively at least), 'I just want to help these people', he concluded (quoted in Hassan, 2013, p 229).

Many of the young men on the trip expressed similar views. They had not appreciated that taken-for-granted food, such as fish and chips and chicken and chips, were simply not available there 'because they do not have it.' Although these young Somali men had known beforehand that life was very different in Somaliland, they were still struck by seeing it for themselves. And by the ways in which young people there were coping, despite lacking basic necessities. 'You know,

I will take this experience: it will be with me for a long period of time', another of them reflected, in conclusion.

Many of these young Somali men returned to London enthusiastically committed to organising practical support for their counterparts back in Somaliland. This could be interpreted as developing transnationalism, building solidarity between young Somali people in very different contexts, across continents. Conversely, however, the development of such ties could be viewed far more negatively, the source of increasing suspicion and fear, against the wider background of the War on Terror.

In summary

This chapter has provided examples to illustrate a variety of ways in which communities have been responding to experiences of displacement as a result of violence. There have been stories of solidarity and mutual support, with ties developing across national boundaries as well as within them. And there have been examples of community development initiatives to support those who have been displaced, to enable them to support each other more effectively. But these initiatives have been affected, and too often undermined, as a result of the wider policy context, just as they have been affected, and too often undermined, as the result of wider prejudices and fears. Subsequent chapters explore some of the potential implications for the development of policies and practices to promote community cohesion and social solidarity for the future.

FOUR

Community responses to displacement as a result of (re)development

'A process of displacement and dispossession', according to David Harvey, 'lies at the core of the urban process under capitalism' (Harvey, 2013, p 18). In the slums of Mumbai, India, in the past, for example, 'financial powers backed by the state, push for forcible slum clearance, in some cases violently taking possession of a terrain occupied by a whole generation of slum-dwellers', he pointed out (although there have been very different experiences too, as will be suggested later). Similar, if less brutal and more legalistic forms of dispossession could be identified in US cities, in his view, displacing long-term residents in reasonable housing in favour of higher-order land uses (such as condominiums) (Harvey, 2013, p 19). Such forms of 'feral capitalism', predatory practices and the dispossession of the poor and vulnerable had become the order of the day, Harvey concluded, making the case for the importance of developing alternatives through popular democratic movements for social transformation.

This chapter focuses on community responses to dispossession and displacement as a result of (re)development. Development has been a contested notion in general, and so has urban redevelopment more specifically. Definitions and approaches differ. And so do communities' responses, depending on their varying interests and aspirations.

In recent years there have been examples of community-based resistance to displacement as a result of development projects in rural contexts in the global South, just as there have been examples of community-based resistance to displacement as a result of urban redevelopment programmes in cities across the globe. In other cases in contrast, however, rather than focusing on resistance per se, communities have developed their own alternative approaches, just as communities, and individuals within communities, have chosen to move on willingly, of their own accord. Chapter Six explores the question of choice and human agency in response to displacement pressures further, while taking account of wider frameworks of structural constraints.

Having identified examples of varying community responses in general, this chapter moves on to focus on examples of community responses to displacement as a result of urban redevelopment more specifically. These particular examples come from London, a global city with correspondingly powerful pressures competing for urban space, as Chapter Two has already explained. The significance of London's role, as capital city/city of capital, sets the background for the discussion of displacement through market forces more generally in Chapter Five, along with the varying impacts of public policy, both locally and beyond.

Development and redevelopment: definitions and approaches

'But what is development?' Foster-Carter questioned in his social development text, before going on to consider a number of the contentious assumptions that he identified as inherent in varying definitions (Foster-Carter, 1989, p 92). Typically, he suggested, the term 'development' was associated with economic growth. But definitions have included social dimensions, too, along with political, cultural and (more recently) ecological dimensions. And each of these has been potentially contentious. The *Oxford dictionary*'s definitions start from the notion of development as a 'gradual unfolding' process, 'a fuller working out' of inherent possibilities, whether these have economic, social, political or cultural dimensions.

So what might such processes of unfolding change involve, and for whose benefit? To what end? Critics have pointed to the Eurocentrism underpinning stages of growth-type approaches – equating development with advancement on the path towards liberal capitalism along Western lines. But what about other possibilities?

International development strategies have been similarly subjected to criticisms from varying perspectives. Neoliberal theorists have questioned the value of intervening to promote development at all. Left to themselves, market forces promote economic growth of their own accord, thereby reducing poverty, while facilitating the development of liberal democracies in the process. Or do they?

Market forces can and do bring change. But with what impact? As Chapter Two has already argued, alternative approaches focus on the underlying structural inequalities that market forces tend to exacerbate, raising questions about who gains even more – and who loses even more – as the result of particular development interventions. Parallel arguments have been similarly applied to urban redevelopment processes – who gains and who loses, whether the results have been consciously planned – or not. Reflecting on government initiatives to tackle urban problems in a variety of contexts, Mike Davis has argued that 'the state intervenes regularly in the name of "progress", "beautification", and even "social justice for the poor"', but that the effects have been 'to redraw spatial boundaries to the advantage of landowners, foreign investors, elite homeowners, and middle-class communities.' As a result, Davis continues, 'The contemporary scale of population removal is immense', concluding by describing the urban poor as 'nomads' as a result (Davis, 2007, p 98).

David Harvey has developed similar arguments about the causes of urban dispossession, locating these within the structural causes of inequality under capitalism (Harvey, 2008). Governments and civil society organisations may well intervene with the intention of addressing poverty and inequality, but if they fail to address the underlying causes, the results may be limited, if not actually counterproductive. Policies to tackle concentrations of urban poverty by promoting greater social mix provide cases in point. As Ley has argued in this context, policies to tackle segregation (racial as well as social segregation) in US cities in the 1960s and 1970s could be seen to start from relatively progressive intentions (Ley, 2012). In more recent times, however, social mixing policies have become associated with gentrification. And gentrification has become associated with the displacement of the urban poor. As Glyn pointed out in the same collection of essays on social mix, gentrification brought benefits to some of the working-class residents of the area that she studied in Dundee, Scotland. Not all were displaced. But many were. Whether intentionally or not, policies to promote redevelopment resulted in deconcentrations of those who were being defined as 'problematised people' (Glyn, 2012), 'removing human encumberments', as the poor were being perceived in other contexts (Davis, 2007, p 98).

Responses to displacement: examples from India

There are numerous examples of resistance to development projects that have threatened to displace local communities. As Dutta and others have argued, displacement can occur 'in the name of progress of the nation', but too often the displaced population has to pay a very heavy price involving not only 'the simple loss and destruction of goods and property, but people's lives and their social ties are also left behind in tatters, giving a final blow to their ultimate source of subsistence' (Dutta, 2007, p xiii). So no wonder that there have been examples of community-based resistance.

In India, for instance, the novelist and activist, Arundhati Roy, has written about campaigns against big dam projects, such as the Narmada Valley project. It was estimated that this would displace some 25,000,000 people living in the valley concerned. While recognising that the statistics have been disputed, she quoted estimates of between 40 million and 50 million people displaced by large dam projects in India overall between Independence and the turn of the 20th century (Roy, 1999). If those displaced by other development projects were included too, she argued, the number would be three times greater than the number of those displaced by the violence that accompanied the Partition of India from Pakistan at the time of Independence.

Roy went on to point out that there were also major environmental effects from big dam projects. Initially The World Bank had apparently been prepared to finance the lynch-pin projects of the Narmada Valley schemes even before both the human and environmental impacts had been costed. Slogans like 'People's dams' sounded so positive, Roy argued, but the realities were turning out very differently. There were ongoing problems of effectiveness, with continuing droughts and floods despite the construction of big dams. And there were other environmental effects. Most importantly, from her perspective, there were major problems of displacement, which were disproportionately affecting the most disadvantaged groups – dalits (previously called 'untouchables') and tribal peoples.

When some construction work began back in 1961, local communities had been unaware of the potential threats. But as the work gathered momentum, they began to see how many people were going to be displaced – and who would benefit. So they started to organise themselves. By 1986 there were people's organisations in the Indian states affected, organisations that started to question officials about their promises of resettlement and rehabilitation. These organisations came together in 1988 to form a single umbrella organisation, the Narmada Bachao Andoloan (NBA), united around the call for all work on the Narmada Valley Development Projects to be stopped until these issues were resolved. They built alliances with friendly organisations elsewhere, including Friends of the Earth in Japan (that pressured their government to withdraw a loan that would have supported the investment). And they mobilised more than 50,000 people to gather in the Narmada Valley itself, in protest.

The government responded with repression, threatening 'to flood the valley with khaki' (Roy, 1999, p 46). But this only led to further escalations of campaigning, including a hunger strike by seven activists in 1991. Meanwhile sympathisers abroad were pressurising The World Bank (one of the key potential funders), leading it to announce that, rather than simply pressing ahead, they were commissioning an independent review of key parts of the overall scheme. This Commission produced its report in 1992, concluding that the projects' resettlement and rehabilitation plans were inadequate, while the environmental impacts had not been properly considered, conclusions that led The World Bank to decide to hold off.

This seemed like an extraordinary victory, as Roy saw it, 'No-one has ever managed to make The World Bank step back from a project before. Least of all a ragtag army of the poorest people in one of the world's poorest countries' (Roy, 1999, p 56). 'Sacking The World Bank was and is a huge moral victory for the people of the valley', she concluded, although 'The euphoria didn't last.' This was far from being the end of the story.

The state government of Gujarat stepped in to fund the shortfall, but campaigning continued. As a result of a writ petition to the Supreme Court, further work on the dam was eventually ordered to be suspended in 1995 on the grounds that the rehabilitation of displaced people had been inadequate. But work on other dams continued.

At the time of writing her book at the end of the 1990s, Roy reflected on the achievements of local communities campaigning together while building support internationally. Changes had been made, but there were still environmental concerns. And the resettlement of displaced people continued to be problematic, to say the very least. Some had been given land, but others hadn't. Some had land that was irretrievably water-logged while others had been given stony, uncultivable land. Some had been driven out by landowners, and some had been robbed, beaten and chased away by their host villagers. There were conflicts over resources – water, grazing land and jobs – and conflicts with a group of landless labourers who had been sharecropping for absentee landlords who had subsequently sold the land to the government.

These dam schemes have been highly controversial. The issues were not about whether such development schemes were potentially desirable per se, but whether they were being effectively planned to deliver the promised development gains. And most importantly, the issues concerned who was to benefit and who was to lose out. However reasonable the claims for resettlement and rehabilitation, in the case of these Narmada schemes, governments had been unable to deliver, Roy concluded. The most disadvantaged people were further disadvantaged as a result, while others were profiting at their expense.

Similar conclusions have been reached by a number of other studies, as the title of one of these illustrates only to clearly – *Big dams, displaced people: Rivers of sorrow, rivers of change* (Thukral, 1992). Not everyone can be absorbed on the land, following such displacement processes, this study concluded, but resettlement and rehabilitation processes needed to include education and training so that people could access other livelihoods. And people needed to be more careful with natural resources, wasting less water and less energy as a result. As Raina and colleagues similarly concluded, there needed to be less greed, and changes to an 'urbanised, elitist, consumerist lifestyle' (Raina et al, 1997, p 137).

The Narmada schemes provide just one set of examples for illustration. Development schemes have been the focus for community campaigning much more widely across India and elsewhere, internationally. Communities have taken on private sector development interests. And they have taken on policy-makers who have supported them, within different structures and levels of government.

In principle, development should be a process of expanding the real freedoms that people enjoy, according to Amartya Sen, removing the unfreedoms associated with poverty, tyranny, exclusion and neglect. But as Newell and Wheeler's collection of studies on *Rights, resources and the politics of accountability* demonstrates, the reality has all too often been very different. Their book explores key questions about how the poor and marginalised can come together to negotiate and claim their rights from the rich and powerful, in varying contexts (Newell and Wheeler, 2006). Newell and his colleagues' own contribution to this collection (Newell et al, 2006) provides illustrations, drawing on three Indian case studies – a thermal power project, an industrial development site (providing space for petrochemical companies, mostly) and a mining project having an impact on tribal communities' lands. Although these cases were different in many respects, there were striking similarities in the ways in which decisions were being made, and in which the affected communities were mobilising to make their voices heard and so protect their interests.

The case studies raised questions about who was entitled to compensation, for example, and who was not. All too often the most disadvantaged groups lacked formal evidence of their rights to the lands in question, and so were unable to claim compensation. There were also questions about environmental impacts on livelihoods, with dust generated by mining activities having an impact on crops, for instance. And there were questions about the potential health hazards for those who were so desperate that they were prepared to work in these projects regardless.

In response, local communities came together to develop alternative People's Development Plans, with the support of local NGOs and a well-respected international NGO, the Society for Participatory Research in Asia (PRIA) (an NGO that I have had the benefit of working with personally, over a number of years). These plans fed into public hearings, enabling communities to share experiences and to learn from each other, identifying the potential risks (such as the risk of water pollution), as well as sharing learning about alternative approaches. The public hearings also provided spaces for dialogue with the companies concerned, although with varying results.

While some communities evidently valued these approaches, others preferred to channel their concerns and grievances through state authorities, here, too, with varying results. The law could be invoked to support community claims for corporate accountability, but it could also be invoked to break up people's protests.

Communities were developing multipronged strategies to secure accountability. There were important lessons here for those concerned to promote community development, facilitating the development of community-based alternatives. There were delicate balances to be struck, if NGOs were to provide the necessary expertise, but without taking over campaigns from the communities themselves. PRIA enjoyed precisely the type of trust that was needed to play such a role, it emerged, providing the necessary expertise and leadership without undermining the communities themselves.

The role of NGOs and community-based organisations has been centrally important in other contexts, too, demonstrating ways in which local people can be supported to make their voices heard more effectively in urban redevelopment processes. The resettlement of the urban poor from railway lands in Mumbai in the 1990s provides a case in point (Burra, 1999). The background to this particular story starts from the arrival of migrants, fleeing from drought and rural poverty in search of better livelihoods in the rapidly growing city of Mumbai. Unable to afford other housing options, these migrants settled in slums, including slums beside the railways, often far too close to the railway tracks for safety. Accidents were all too frequent as a result, disastrous for the families concerned as well as very distressing for the train drivers involved. This was causing problems and delays all round.

Eventually, in 1998, the relevant authorities came together to agree on a plan to resettle the families living beside one of these main rail tracks, aiming to achieve this in a low-cost and participatory way, thereby developing a model for future redevelopment initiatives elsewhere. Given that the state government lacked experience of the type of participatory resettlement programmes that The World Bank was by then advocating for urban redevelopment programmes as well as for rural development initiatives, it was decided to appoint the Society for the Promotion of Area Resource Centers (SPARC), an Indian NGO with a relevant record, to facilitate this as a participatory resettlement project. So, working in partnership with other trusted organisations, SPARC engaged local residents in participatory mapping of the existing settlement, before enabling households to plan how they would prefer to be relocated, choosing whether or not to stay next to their previous neighbours when they moved to their new homes close by, thereby preserving community networks in the process.

Residents then grouped themselves into 27 housing cooperative societies, which provided the basis for future developments, as temporary shelters were to be improved over time. And women's participation was given specific priority throughout. By May 1999, all 900 of the families who were to be resettled had been successfully relocated – on target and without any law and order problems in the process. People had moved voluntarily, without forcible removals or demolitions, thereby demonstrating what could be achieved by genuinely participatory processes, facilitated by trusted community-based organisations and NGOs (Burra, 1999). This provided a model that could be replicated elsewhere.

In other Indian contexts, too, communities have developed their own strategies for community engagement and subsequent survival when finally faced with the effects of displacement. On a practice exchange tour in India, organised by the International Association for Community Development in 2012, a group of us visited a range of such initiatives, learning from the ways in which communities had been coming together in response to the loss of grazing lands, and the side effects of dam schemes, for example. We visited women's micro-credit schemes. And we visited community projects, building on traditional knowledge and skills to develop sustainable livelihoods while meeting social needs. The visits included a trip to a project that was researching and developing the use of indigenous plants for medicinal purposes. As subsequent reflections on these visits recorded, the visitors had appreciated communities' energies and commitment, together with the continuing contributions of community-based leadership and community and NGO-based support structures (see www.iacdglobal. org/practitioner-dialogue-2012/rural-visits).

Examples from Brazil

The Landless People's Movement (Movimento dos Trabalhadores Sem Terra in Portuguese, or MST) in Brazil provides another such case study of community development responses to displacement. From the 1960s small farmers and rural workers in Brazil faced displacement as a result of the then military government's strategy to promote agricultural modernisation. Small-scale production was devastated as a result. The impacts were massive, with the loss of some 10,000 jobs in the agricultural sector between 1985 and 1995, and a further 4 million people abandoning the agricultural sector between 1995 and 1999 (Vergara-Camus, 2014). In total, according to Martinez-Torres and Firmiano, more than 50,000,000 people left the countryside between 1960 and 2000 (Martinez-Torres and Firmiano, 2016).

Many of those displaced moved to the city, only to face different forms of marginalisation there as they competed for the jobs that were all too scarce. Meanwhile, many of those who did remain as small farmers faced their own struggles for survival in the countryside. It was these two groups, the rural dispossessed and the urban unemployed, who formed the basis for the Landless People's Movement. This set out to establish community-based alternatives – from the bottom up.

The MST grew out of the self-organisation of working families and the occupation of territory by landless families. Groups of between 20 and 100 families would come together and set up a base camp from which to occupy a particular piece of land in order to establish a rural community, promoting community-based development from the bottom up. Once there, negotiations would start in order to obtain legal rights. Sometimes these clusters of families succeeded straight away. But often it took a number of attempts before they managed to establish themselves on the land, having initially faced eviction, whether by the police or by the gunmen who had been hired by local landowners.

As Martinez-Torres and Firmiano went on to explain, people spoke of the difficulties of those early days, a period of suffering and struggle that could nevertheless serve to strengthen people's determination. Even if people started out as individuals and families, they came together, as communities, through these processes of struggle. And so, Martinez-Torres and Firmiano concluded, 'the camps become spaces for education and training' (2016, p 156).

In the early days there were high levels of participation, it seemed, as groups organised themselves in clusters. These formed the basis for community decision-making on all aspects of daily life, coordinated by a General Assembly for the camp. Initially there were attempts to form collectives, producing cooperatively too. But cooperative production was apparently not for everyone.

Still much was achieved, cooperatively. Families did manage to build a sense of community, working together to campaign for key services such as schools, healthcare and safe drinking water. And they developed services such as community education for themselves, collectively. In Vergara-Camus' view these movements (in Brazil as elsewhere in Latin America) were providing islands of alternative approaches to development, posing potential challenges to the neoliberal approaches that were so predominant more generally. The movements were potentially empowering communities (although there were questions concerning the extent to which women were being empowered as well as men). And they were providing learning opportunities for the longer term as communities came to experience power through community education and development processes.

Despite the limitations, Vergara-Camus and Martinez-Torres and Firmiano's accounts both acknowledge MST's achievements. The living conditions of settler families were improved through community development approaches. Alliances were built, including with progressive political parties, locally and regionally, but without jeopardising MST's autonomy (Vergara-Camus, 2014; Martinez-Torres and Firmiano, 2016). And alternative, more sustainable approaches to development were being promoted, expanding the use of agro-ecological techniques. These were to be contrasted with the less sustainable approaches of capitalised agribusinesses, supported as they were by international finance.

There were limitations to be acknowledged too, however. Much still needed to be done. These were still no more than islands, pockets where community development alternatives were being promoted around the need for common services for social reproduction, even if they struggled to include more collective approaches to production per se. And despite building alliances locally, and developing links with international movements (including links with La Via Campesina, an international movement promoting sustainable family farming), MST has been described as being unable to construct an explicitly anti-neoliberal bloc, more widely, on a global scale (Vergara-Camus, 2014). The inherent limitations of locally based approaches re-emerge in subsequent chapters together with the potential importance of alliance building more generally.

Responses in urban redevelopment contexts

As the example of the MST in Brazil illustrates, communities have shared experiences of displacement and they have identified common interests in response, even if they have struggled to build wider blocs, committed to developing alternative approaches, across urban–rural divides. Urban redevelopment schemes can pose just as many challenges as rural development schemes, raising similar questions as to who gains the most and who stands to lose the most from market-driven strategies for development and change. Here, too, in urban contexts, even the best intentioned of schemes can backfire, bringing displacement rather than more desirable living conditions for the most disadvantaged social groups.

Race and ethnicity have been key factors here, as well as caste and social class. Racial displacement has a long and violent history, as indigenous First Nation communities have been dispossessed by those who have effectively occupied their spaces, from way back in colonial times. Both established communities and newer arrivals have been displaced in other contexts, too, apartheid South Africa providing particularly brutal examples, separating black from white and Indian from 'coloured' or mixed race communities. The photographs taken by Bryan Heseltine in 1950s Cape Town included records of areas such as District Six, areas from which mixed communities were to be forcibly displaced, to make way for an exclusively white population (Newbury, 2013). Although he was himself white, Heseltine would seem to have succeeded in gaining the trust of the communities that he portrayed, judging from the evidence of the photographs themselves. These photographs were subsequently displayed, at St Martin in the Fields, London, in 1955, testifying to the vitality of mixed township communities while raising awareness and support for campaigning against their traumatic dislocations as the result of apartheid redevelopment (Newbury, 2013).

Apartheid South Africa provides an extreme example of displacement by violence. But urban regeneration schemes can also result – and have resulted – in racial displacements by very different means. And sometimes, as already suggested, displacement has been the result of policies that have been promoted with the very best intentions. For example, Bob Fisher's account of neighbourhood organising in the US explains the links between poverty and race together with the links between neighbourhood organising and the Civil Rights movement, with racial desegregation a key objective of both (Fisher, 1994).

The modernisation of agriculture in the southern states in the post-Second World War period resulted in massive displacement for African Americans, who had then moved to the cities of the north in search of alternative livelihoods. Once there, however, they had experienced continuing poverty and new forms of deprivation in these northern urban ghettoes, problems that were to be addressed by urban redevelopment and community development schemes. Except that such schemes failed to take sufficient account of the underlying structures of inequality, including inequalities of race as well as social class.

As Fisher explained, there were neighbourhoods, including white working-class neighbourhoods, as well as African American and Hispanic neighbourhoods in large cities, 'that experienced serious deterioration and displacement by the mid-1970s' because of a number of factors including urban renewal and the gentrification that followed, as a result (Fisher, 1994, p 156). In other words, urban redevelopment was actually compounding the problems of these areas rather than resolving them, as the contemporary slogan 'Urban renewal equals negro removal' reflected. There were examples of community-based resistance, in response, however, with hundreds of neighbourhood organisations mobilising to fight renewal in this period.

Since then, from the latter part of the 20th century onwards, community organisations have continued to resist urban regeneration schemes in varying contexts. As Jewison and Macgregor's collection of essays demonstrated, for example, cities of the advanced capitalist world were being transformed from this period, generating a series of crises and conflicts in the process (Jewison and Macgregor, 1997). From Vancouver and San Francisco on the west coast of the Americas, to inner-city Birmingham in Britain, communities were resisting the threat of displacement, attempting to minimise the disadvantages and maximise the potential benefits of urban (re)development (Beazley et al, 1997). Whatever their efforts, however, Beazley and his colleagues concluded that generally 'community groups are no match for powerful development interests and growth coalitions', while supposedly democratically accountable local government authorities prioritise pro-growth interests above the needs of the disadvantaged communities to which they should be accountable (Beazley et al, 1997, p 191).

Public policies, at both local and central government levels, re-emerge as key factors in subsequent chapters. How far do public policies prioritise the interests of developers, promoting market-driven strategies for social change? Or conversely, how far do public policies commit to meeting social needs rather than to maximising private profits? Changes in the balance of power, as between the state and the market, emerge as key factors here, in the British context.

Before moving on to explore community responses to urban redevelopment in contemporary London, however, one further point needs to be re-emphasised. Communities can and do have differences within them as well as between them. People can and do have different interests, and may come to different conclusions about how these interests are best served when faced with urban redevelopment proposals. While some may be resistant to potential threats of dispersal, others may prefer to leave. Dispersal may seem the best option in terms of obtaining better housing elsewhere, for example. The compensation on offer may be attractive, too. Or people may actually choose to leave in order to join families and communities elsewhere.

There are international as well as more local examples. Aravind Adiga's novel, *Last man in tower*, provides a fictional account of such differences in the context of urban redevelopment in contemporary Mumbai, India (Adiga, 2011). The property developer in question aims to tear down a weathered tower block, replacing this with more profitable apartments. As the story progresses, more and more of the residents come to accept the compensation that is being offered, seeing this as being in their own best interests, until only one resident stands out, refusing to be displaced. Conflicts are exacerbated as a result – with potentially predictable consequences for those who refuse to cooperate.

Community responses to redevelopment in contemporary London

As Chapter Two has already pointed out, 21st-century London exemplifies the contemporary world city (Massey, 2007). As banking, together with related industries and services, has been expanding in the global financial city of capital (Sassen, 2007), so has competition for urban space. London has been growing in population, with increasing social polarisation between the seriously wealthy on the one hand, and the most marginal on the other, including newcomers as well as longer-established communities. This unequal competition for space has been compounded by reductions in the supply of genuinely affordable housing. Although by no means confined to London, this housing crisis has been particularly acute in the capital city.

The lack of genuinely affordable housing has been a growing problem, particularly in inner London areas, as the existing stock of social housing has been reducing (through tenants' rights to buy) without sufficient replacements, let alone sufficient replacements to meet increasing housing needs. Meanwhile, those on low incomes – and increasingly those on average incomes too – have been unable to afford to buy their own homes, typically leaving them with no alternative but to rent from private landlords. Too many have been finding themselves forced to pay half, or even more, of their incomes on rent – for too often poorly maintained properties and without security of tenure. Chapter Five goes into more detail, exploring the toxic effects of market forces combined with market-led public policies towards housing and planning more generally. A brief summary is all that is needed here, for the purposes of this particular chapter, focusing on the impacts of redevelopment schemes more specifically.

The housing crisis has been bearing on the least advantaged groups in society most harshly, newcomers and longer-established communities alike. The problems have been particularly marked for people with disabilities and women who have been subjected to domestic violence, as changes in housing policies have been compounded by social welfare reforms. But the housing crisis has been increasingly having an impact on wider social groupings too, as young professionals find themselves forced to share rooms with strangers in privately rented flats, moving on every six months or so when their tenancies run out (Mayo and Newman, 2014). Unsurprisingly, then, given the extent of London's housing crisis, housing redevelopment schemes have been contentious to say the least. Who would stand to gain, and who might stand to lose as a result?

In the past, redevelopment schemes have been criticised for breaking up existing communities (Young and Willmott, 2007), and for promoting gentrification in their place. But redevelopment schemes have also provided better housing and security of tenure. In the post-Second World War period, council housing was to provide homes for those who had been displaced by the bombing, along with others in housing need. Aneurin Bevan, one of the key architects of the welfare state that was being developed at the time, was a man with a vision for these new estates – aiming to rebuild the mixed communities of the past 'where the doctor, the grocer, the butcher and the farm labourer all lived in the same street' (cited in Foot, 1973, p 76). While some tenants were reluctant to move to these new estates, others were actually delighted with their new homes – whether or not they quite matched up to Bevan's vision for the future of council housing.

In the contemporary context, however, this all seems so distant. The risks of redevelopment loom larger, with fears that such schemes would lead inexorably on to 'social cleansing' as the result. Reviewing the situation in 2015, Gerald Koessl and I produced a report on the loss of social housing that was accompanying such development schemes in London, together with policy recommendations for a future government (this being a pre-election period) (Koessl and Mayo, 2015). A London Assembly Housing Committee report, published earlier in 2015 (London Assembly Housing Committee, 2015), had already identified significant losses of genuinely affordable homes as the result of estate redevelopment, or 'estate regeneration', the term that was being used to describe these types of property development.

Our report updated this further. London's households had increased by 11% between 2004 and 2014, but the stock of social housing had been failing to keep up, with actual declines in almost half of the local authorities concerned, across the city. Even local authorities that were committed to building more social housing were struggling financially, just as they were struggling to find the resources to maintain their existing estates. Unsurprisingly, then, there were attractions to the possibilities of regenerating social housing estates in partnership with developers. Some of the refurbished homes could then be sold on privately, for profit, thereby providing the resources with which to refurbish the rest.

In principle, such schemes need not necessarily have entailed major reductions in the social housing stock. Densities could be increased, for example, thereby maintaining the stock of social housing alongside the new developments. But in practice, estate regeneration schemes were all too often leading to the loss of social housing and the consequent dispersal of social housing tenants. Those who had bought their leases were also potentially at risk of dispersal, as they themselves discovered, if the compensation on offer proved inadequate in terms of finding affordable alternatives in the area.

The numbers involved were significant. Between 2004 and 2014, estate redevelopment schemes in London led to the loss of some 8,296 socially rented homes, leading to problems of dispersal that were increasing as we wrote. This was the context for community campaigns against redevelopment in London.

There are so many stories of community campaigns against development proposals – on varying grounds. There may be objections for environmental reasons, for instance, or objections on aesthetic grounds (the proposed developments being considered too ugly, or too intrusive, blocking out desirable views). Others object to virtually any form of development in their immediate neighbourhoods – proponents of 'NIMBYism' or 'not in my back yard'. These stories have their places in community histories, of course. But they are not the subject of this particular chapter. The case studies that follow focus more specifically on community campaigns to resist displacement – social cleansing as a result of estate redevelopment schemes.

Focus E15

Focus E15 is a much quoted example of a successful campaign, waged by a group of residents from a hostel in Stratford, East London. The hostel had been providing 210 flats, with accommodation for young people under 25 with support needs, including those coming out of social services care and those having become homeless as a result of suffering from domestic violence. In 2013 a group of young mothers came together when faced with the threat of eviction from their housing association landlord. Seeking information from the local authority, they were advised simply to look for alternative accommodation before the date of the eviction, in the private sector. If they were unable to find accommodation within the limits of the benefits system by 20 October 2013, the local authority would find them accommodation outside London in Manchester, Hastings or Birmingham (where rents might be more realistically affordable than in London).

This shocked the women concerned. They were, in their own words "angered and outraged". The campaign began in earnest, with a regular street stall in the local shopping centre. More direct action followed, including occupations of both the housing association's offices and the council's offices, along with the occupation of a block of empty flats on an almost totally abandoned council estate, nearby, under the shadow of the Olympic stadium. They were simply not prepared to put up with being squeezed out when they could be rehoused within the borough. "How could a council turn away its own residents in order to facilitate more upmarket developments?", they asked the mayor.

The mayor's reactions to them had further outraged the mothers who had felt that they were being treated dismissively, with disrespect, as they subsequently explained to me. He had expressed the view that, "if you can't afford to live in Newham, you can't afford to live in Newham." This had increased their determination to hold the council responsible.

In Focus E15's view, the problem was that their borough was "becoming a place for only the rich!" Property development in the area had been stimulated by the building and improved transport infrastructure that had been taking place for the London Olympic Games in 2012. Property prices had been rising, as a result of these developments, with ripple effects that were only too clear to see. "We must not let this happen", Focus E15 continued. "Homes should be for living not for profit" . "Social cleansing needs to stop!" "Social housing not social cleansing, housing is a right, here to stay, here to fight." (From Focus E15 website, http://focus15.org/ [URL no longer active])

Far from being a long-established community, Focus E15 only came together as a community when faced with the common threat of eviction. But their determination made up for their lack of prior experiences of working together as a group. Rather than being dispersed across the country, they were all rehoused more locally in the borough, as a result.

This was a remarkable achievement in itself. As a journalist reflected in 2014, 'Focus E15 Mums have fought for the right to a home', showing 'the true worth of grassroots protest' (Kwei, 2014). They were described as being articulate and resourceful, drawing on support from others, including celebrities with media contacts – without allowing this to undermine their own community-based leadership. But they themselves were only too conscious of the limitations of their victory. They were all rehoused in privately rented accommodation, facing the threat of soaring rents and short-term tenancies for the future. This was a very precarious situation for the mothers involved and for their children, still subject to the vagaries of market forces.Some two years after this report, in 2016, I met with a group of the Focus E15 mothers and their supporters at their regular street stall. They had been continuing to run this stall by the local shopping centre, on Saturday mornings, ever since their campaign had begun, some three years back. The stall was very visible, with brightly coloured posters, so that people could – and did – know where to find them, coming up to the stall in search of advice and support. And the stall was very audible, with music blaring out between the open microphone sessions.

Some of those who spoke were clearly accustomed to speaking in public, explaining the challenges that were being posed by the latest Housing and Planning legislation, informing people of the threats that this would pose to their future security, as tenants and residents. The open microphone sessions were about building campaigning, mobilising communities as well as informing them. But they were also about supporting individuals and their families, I was told, enabling people to gain the knowledge and the confidence to speak up for themselves – hence the ways in which people were being encouraged to take up the microphone for themselves, to have their say.

The stall was next to the stall of a campaigning political group, the Revolutionary Communist Group. This had been very important, the local mothers explained, because this group had provided them with the very basic organisational resources that they had needed when they had first come together, resources such as access to printing facilities to run off their leaflets. The group had been inviting the mothers to speak at their stall, which they still stand beside in their street work every Saturday. This backing had been crucial, they explained, enabling them to build their campaign, making the links between the different aspects of the effects of social cleansing. For example, a local teacher told me that she had become involved as she had come to realise the impact of the housing crisis on her pupils – with constant moves from one insecure tenancy to another.

Nearly three years on, Focus E15 had become a well-recognised local presence, combining support for individuals with campaigning against social cleansing more widely, as I witnessed when I visited on several occasions. They had acquired the use of a shop opposite the market stall as a base, named 'Sylvia's Corner' to commemorate Sylvia Pankhurst, the socialist feminist who had contributed so much to community campaigning in East London in the past.

Reflecting on the 80th anniversary of the heroic struggles of Jewish women and girls resisting fascists in the Battle of Cable Street in 1936, Nadia Valman drew comparisons with more contemporary struggles, with migrants once again being blamed for problems with jobs – and housing. 'Reflecting on that extraordinary moment of solidarity in October 1936 [when Jewish women were supported by non-Jewish women, along with dockers and progressive political activists] need not just be an exercise in nostalgia', she argued. 'East London today, a vortex of gentrification, austerity and social exclusion, is also experiencing a renaissance of grassroots protests that carries forward the legacy of Cable Street', she continued. 'The creative resourcefulness of feminist groups like Focus E15 and Sisters Uncut is markedly reminiscent of anarchist and socialist activists in the early twentieth century, who understood locality as the place where social divisions could be challenged and overcome' (Valman, 2016).

Other examples

There are other examples that illustrate the varying experiences of community campaigns against displacement. As in the case of Focus E15, the tenants and residents of the Sweets Way Estate in Barnet, North London, came together when the local authority sold the estate to a developer who planned to demolish 142 social rented homes in order to replace them with more upmarket private dwellings. The tenants and residents campaigned to stop the demolition, halt the evictions of current residents, and offer decanted residents the right to return to their former homes at genuinely affordable rents.

Despite active campaigning, including demonstrations and a massive petition, the evictions continued. By September 2015 only one resident remained, a wheelchair user. When his case came up in court, two of those who had been demonstrating outside the courtroom in his support were arrested.

There seemed little if any remaining scope for negotiation or compromise. Activists had been arguing that "regeneration doesn't have to mean social cleansing." At least it shouldn't, although this was precisely the eventual outcome (previously featured at www.change. org/p/annigton-barnet-homes-stop-the-demolition-of-the-sweets-way-estate [URL no longer active]). But other campaigns have had more success.

The case of the Heygate Estate, in the Elephant and Castle area in South London, provided another much quoted example of community-based resistance to estate regeneration. Following up press accounts of this community's experiences, in the autumn of 2015 I met with one of the local activists, Jerry Flynn, who filled me in on their story.

Jerry had been brought up on the estate himself. His family had moved there in 1974, rehoused from an overcrowded, privately rented flat nearby, a flat that had lacked a separate bathroom, let alone central heating. So this move had massively improved the family's housing conditions. Local authority housing (re)developments *could* be beneficial, even if this has been more problematic in more recent times.

Meanwhile, many of those who had moved on to the estate had originally come from relatively nearby too. So there had been some sense of community, right from the start. Overall, in fact, there had been very positive aspects to life on the estate, in Jerry's view. Although the estate had eventually acquired a certain amount of stigma over the years, he explained, this really hadn't been such a problem area at all. Many residents were actually attached to the Heygate, and wanted to stay there. This was the background against which proposals for redevelopment began to be mooted, around 1999/2000.

As it turned out, to cut this story short, the local authority contracted with private developers to knock the existing flats down, with the aim of rebuilding the estate at greater density. 'Affordable' homes would then be made available to existing tenants, who would have the option of moving back on to the estate if they so wished, once the new flats were available. So far, so good, in terms of safeguarding the interests of the local community.

Or was it? As the plans developed, so did the local community's concerns. Heygate Against Transfer (HEAT) was formed by local activists as a result. This was when Jerry himself became involved (in 2004). By this time he was actually living nearby in the surrounding neighbourhood. But close family members and friends *were* still there on the estate, and Jerry shared their concerns as part of the community.

HEAT itself was relatively short-lived as a group, but many of those who had been involved re-emerged and joined with others to form a new group, the Elephant Amenity Network (EAN). Despite EAN's attempts to raise people's concerns, however, the situation was actually deteriorating.

Poster with added local comments

LOCAL PEOPLE
Can you help
'unlock the
Massive
Economic potential of
The Elephant
& Castle area'

By pissing off please.

(Source: Wellcome Library@elenacarter17//e.carter@wellcome.ac.uk)

EAN had been formed in response to local concerns about the redevelopment's likely impact in relation to green space and cycle routes. These became important demands alongside the tenants' key demand for affordable housing, so that existing tenants could afford to stay in the area. They were also committed to campaigning for transparency, to ensure that local communities benefited – and were seen to benefit – from the redevelopment process more generally.

By 2007, it was becoming clear that people were going to be moved off the estate, whatever, with no guarantees in terms of their subsequent rights to return. "People were thoroughly fed up" as a result, Jerry explained, "feeling betrayed, really angry and disappointed." This was when campaigning really began to take off in earnest, in his view.

As the campaign developed, leaseholders began to get involved as well. This was because it was becoming clear that the level of compensation that they were to be offered would be unlikely to be sufficient. So they were also at risk of being unable to afford alternative homes in the neighbourhood. In any case, prices were rising as the result of the redevelopment process itself. And the developers were pushing for further changes to the original plans, changes that could further increase the potential profits of the scheme as a whole.

Meanwhile, further issues were emerging in relation to the 25% of new homes that were to be for affordable rents. The term 'affordable' could actually mean up to 80% of market rents. In this particular case, the developers agreed to limit 'affordable' rents to 50% of the market rent – but even this would be effectively unaffordable for tenants in an inner London area like this. So these were no more than very partial victories for local communities.

The campaign succeeded in challenging the ways in which estate regeneration was being presented and discussed at that time. Activists were highly successful in gaining publicity in the mainstream media, putting across their arguments about the dangers that market-led approaches to urban redevelopment were posing for local communities. They succeeded in making the case for alternative approaches to meet social needs. And most importantly, they succeeded in gaining some concessions for local people in the process.

But the actual number of homes for social rent was disappointing to say the least. Only 79 of the dwellings would be *genuinely* affordable (a figure that subsequently increased to 82), and only 212 of the 2,535 flats (a figure that subsequently increased to 2,704 units) would be 'affordable' as officially categorised (that is, up to 80% market rents and so unaffordable for most of the existing tenants). This had to be set against the total of 1,194 socially rented units being destroyed on the Heygate Estate. Some people might be able to afford to stay, for the longer term, but the rest were being squeezed out, socially cleansed as the result of market forces – led by developers who were working in partnership with the local authority in question.

This last point, about the role of the relevant local authority, highlights contemporary challenges for community development and for social movements more generally too. In neoliberal policy contexts, local authorities face their own challenges and dilemmas that have been exacerbated through the recent imposition of austerity budgets. The scope for local authorities to develop alternative approaches has been correspondingly reduced. But this is absolutely not to accept Margaret Thatcher's much quoted view that 'There is no alternative' to neoliberalism, with no room for manoeuvre at all. On the contrary, there have been choices to be made, for better or for worse, in terms of the interests of local communities, as subsequent chapters will suggest.

Meanwhile, as he reflected on the campaign, Jerry drew attention to a number of lessons to be shared. Despite the challenges, this had been a good campaign in many ways, in his view, with big meetings voicing strong objections from the local community. And there had been some specific gains as the result of some imaginative campaigning. For example, the environmental group Forest Bank, allied to EAN and local Green activists, had managed to save some trees and gain some interim uses, for example, for gardening.

Despite the fact that there had been such powerful campaigning, however, in the end, the developers' planning applications had eventually been approved by the local authority concerned. Still the campaign had held together overall, even when faced with potential tensions and dilemmas (for example, as to how far to cooperate and when to engage with consultations with developers and planners).

More specifically, there had been a determined and successful campaign around gaining access to information on the issue of 'viability'. As already suggested, the developers had been claiming that their scheme would only be viable with less social housing. But they had refused to divulge the basis of the calculations that were being used in support of their arguments. So there followed a determined campaign to obtain the information in question, in order to enable the group to present a convincing challenge to the developers' claims.

This aspect of the campaign involved making a Freedom of Information request to the local authority in question, a request that was initially refused on grounds of commercial confidentiality. But with the support of a lawyer acting for the campaigners on a pro bono basis, this decision was eventually overturned. After three years of active campaigning on this issue in total, the group finally obtained the information that was needed in order to challenge the developers' viability assessments.

This had been a very determined part of the campaign, trying every avenue to obtain the information that was needed in order to challenge the developers' arguments. The fact that the campaign had already gained so much publicity and public interest had also been a contributory factor, adding to their credibility, and so lending weight to their arguments concerning the viability question. This had actually been a key victory – with implications and lessons for other campaigns facing similar arguments from developers claiming that the inclusion of genuinely affordable housing would undermine the viability of their redevelopment schemes. The viability issue itself had been a relatively technical question, of course, rather than a mass campaigning issue per se. But the campaign did still succeed in maintaining mass support locally. This remained firmly rooted in the local community, building unity, including unity between tenants and leaseholders campaigning around their shared objectives.

Jerry also emphasised the importance of the contributions of those with specialist knowledge and skills. Knowledge about the processes involved in making planning applications had been extremely valuable, for instance, along with expert knowledge about Freedom of Information processes. He had also shared his own knowledge and understanding of local government decision-making processes more generally. The group had learned as they went along, as well as learning from others, and sharing this learning with other groups facing similar challenges over redevelopment initiatives in turn.

Others have also been making progress. For example, through determined campaigning, tenants and residents succeeded in persuading the Secretary of State for Communities to refuse to allow the compulsory purchase of flats on the latest phase of neighbouring Aylesbury Estate's redevelopment. This has been hailed as a victory against dispersal for the local community. And tenants on the Butterfield Estate in East London have succeeded in resisting attempts to evict them in order to sell the estate on for more profitable uses in this rapidly gentrifying area. 'The worst thing in the world is to have an insecure roof, and live daily under the constant threat of having to move. Being thrown onto the streets is a horrible prospect', campaigners explained (quoted in Waltham Forest Socialist Party, 2016, p 3). This victory was blazing a trail, they argued, contributing towards the dream of security of tenure more generally.

Reflecting on community-based responses to (re)development more generally

The impact of (re)development has a long history, in London as elsewhere, just as there is a long history of community-based resistance. Writing *Dombey and Son* in 1848, Dickens included a characteristically vivid description of the disruption caused by the coming of the railways through Camden Town (an area, ironically, facing potential disruption from high speed railway developments in the contemporary context). The 'yet unfinished and unopened Railroad was in progress', Dickens explained, 'and from the very core of all this dire disorder, trailed smoothly away, upon its mighty course of civilisation and improvement.' Meanwhile, more sceptical locals regarded the area as:

> ... a sacred grove not to be withered by railroads; and so confident were they generally of its long outliving any such ridiculous inventions, that the master chimney sweeper at the corner, who was understood to take the lead in the local politics of the Garden, had publicly declared that on the occasion of the Railroad opening, if it ever did open, two of his boys should ascend the flues of his dwelling, with instructions to hail the failure with derisive jeers from the chimney pots. (Dickens, 1848 [2012], pp 76-7)

Community-based resistance to (re)development schemes have been varied, but a number of common themes do seem to be emerging from more recent experiences, from both rural and urban contexts, internationally. There have been genuine gains for communities as a result, even if they have too often fallen far short of local communities' original aspirations. And concessions have been won, even if they have been relatively limited, gaining the right to being moved on to a stony plot of land, for instance, or being rehoused in the area but without security of housing tenure. As Davis and Harvey and others have been arguing, market-led development processes tend to result in very unequal benefits (Davis, 2007; Harvey, 2008).

Where communities have made the most effective impacts, this has tended to be the result of very determined campaigning, often extended over very considerable time periods. Communities evidently need stamina as well as determination. In addition, community campaigns have clearly benefited from the support of allies, including international allies in some cases. In fact, building effective alliances has been key. And so has the support of those with particular expertise, including research expertise, shared with communities, without taking over their campaigns in the process – experts on tap rather than experts on top. Communities have been learning from such experts, as well as developing their own processes of learning and sharing with others in solidarity.

None of this is to suggest that communities have been able to disregard the pressures from underlying structural constraints, however. Rather, the point to emphasise is simply this, that there are choices to be made, and alternative strategies to be developed.

FIVE

Responses to displacement via market forces more generally

Eviction is the last refuge for poor tenants
(Headline from *The Guardian*, 18 February 2016)

'A social housing victory, not social cleansing...'

'People power works'

(#NewEraEstate, 19 December 2014)

Communities have organised in response to a variety of displacement pressures, whether as the result of violence or development interventions (however well-intentioned or not, as the case may be). But as Chapter Three has already suggested, dispossession and displacement can have less evident causes, too, reflecting that 'Poverty and exclusion as well as bullets and bombs, cause injury and death, so that oppressive conditions are with good cause sometimes termed "violence" – indirect, impersonal or institutional violence' (Cockburn, 2012, p 3).

This chapter focuses on community responses to such less direct forms of violence. As Chapter Four has already shown, market forces can result in processes of displacement as a result of development and urban redevelopment schemes, whether these schemes involve forcible evictions – or not. Legal procedures can result in dispossession too, with or without the intervention of bailiffs.

This chapter explores the impact of market forces more generally. The discussion starts from community-based resistance to displacement in the past, experiences that have included rent strikes and squatting. These form the background to more recent struggles against displacement via market forces, too often powerfully re-enforced rather than challenged by public policy interventions. Here, too, as in the previous chapter, London, as the capital city/world city of capital, provides particularly extreme examples.

Marketisation processes have been intensifying competition for dwindling supplies of genuinely affordable housing, potentially exacerbating tensions within and between communities as a result. The dangers associated with such situations have been all too evident, especially when they have been exploited for political gain. Without in any way underestimating the challenges involved, however, this chapter includes examples that illustrate the scope for alternative approaches, building solidarity in the face of common threats.

The chapter concludes by reflecting on activists' learning from their experiences of resistance, whether these were experiences of resistance to development/urban redevelopment initiatives, the focus of the previous chapter, or experiences of resistance to market forces more generally, the focus of this particular chapter. What might be the implications for wider understandings of market forces and how can the challenges that they pose be addressed? And how might such understandings relate to more theoretical analyses of market forces and the scope for state interventions and for community action to mitigate their effects (Esping-Andersen, 1985; Harvey, 2013; Sassen, 2014; Farnsworth and Irving, 2015)?

Community-based resistance in the recent past

There have been examples of resistance to displacement as a result of market forces from way back in the past. Prebble's account of the Highland Clearances tells the story of how farmers were betrayed by their own chiefs in 18th-century Scotland, for instance. People were displaced from their homes to make way for more profitable, but less labour-intensive, forms of agricultural production, sheep farming (Prebble, 1963). Those who resisted were eventually driven out 'with bayonet, truncheon and fire' (their homes were torched). While their chiefs 'grew rich on meat and wool, the people died of cholera and starvation or, evicted from the glens to make way for sheep, were forced to emigrate to foreign lands', Prebble explains.

Would those who arrived in Nova Scotia, Canada and elsewhere be categorised as refugees or economic migrants, according to more recent definitions – or both, perhaps? As Barrington Moore's study of the development of modern capitalism argued, both the agrarian and industrial revolutions and the development of modern capitalism emerged from histories of violence – direct and/or indirect – followed by wide-scale displacements as a result (Moore, 1966).

Ellen Meiksins Wood's account of the development of capitalism tells a similar story of the 'evils' of the 'collateral damage of "modernization"' (Meiksins Wood, 1991, p 161). While recognising that capitalism had certainly 'produced unprecedented advances in material well-being', she went on to point out that 'waste, deprivation, cultural degradation and an irrational distribution of labour and resources are the products of the same systemic imperatives' of capitalist development (Meiksins

Wood, 1991, p 165) – including histories of displacement, from earlier times, through the enclosures when 'sheep devoured men'.

In more recent times, the shortage of genuinely affordable housing has been the trigger for community-based resistance to threats of displacement in Britain. There have been examples of squatting movements, for instance, and rent strikes in protest at the imposition of rent increases where these have been perceived as being unaffordable and unfair – with the accompanying risks of eviction and displacement as a result.

One of the best known of these community-based resistance struggles was the Glasgow rent strike, during the First World War. As Nan Milton, the daughter of one of the key activists, John Maclean, explained, the background to this struggle was as follows. Since the beginning of the war, thousands of workers had flooded into Glasgow to work in the munitions factories, causing the demand for housing in some districts to be much greater than the supply as a result. The munitions workers were relatively better paid (their labour being much in demand, in wartime). So, realising that they could charge the munitions workers more, landlords began to raise the rents. But this posed affordability problems for the wives and families of the soldiers and sailors who were away fighting (Milton, 1973).

When one landlord demanded a second increase, tenants began to organise themselves for resistance (with support from a progressive local councillor), agreeing to pay the regular rent but refusing to pay the increase. The women led a movement 'such as had never been seen before, or since for that matter', in the view of another activist from that time, Willie Gallacher. 'Street meetings, back-court meetings, drums, bells, trumpets – every method was used to bring the women out and organize them for the struggle', he continued. 'In street after street, scarcely a window without one [that is, a notice saying] "We are not paying increased rent"' (Gallacher, 1978, pp 52-3).

The landlords proceeded to apply to the courts in order to evict their rent-striking tenants, although this was easier said than done. According to Gallacher, the women could 'smell a sheriff's officer a mile away'. So before the sheriffs were anywhere near the home of the tenant who was to be evicted, 'the officer and his men would be met by an army of furious women who drove them back in a hurried scramble for safety.... The increased rent could not be collected, the tenants could not be evicted' (Gallacher, 1978, pp 52-3).

When the landlords attempted different legal tactics (to collect the rent increases from the tenants' wages, at source) this was met with further resistance. This time the men who were working in the munitions factories staged walkouts in solidarity with the women rent strikers, creating panic among the authorities concerned as a result. 'The workers have left the factories', the sheriff explained, in an urgent phone call to the Minister of Munitions, Lloyd George. 'What am I to do?' 'Stop the case', he was told in reply. 'A Rent Restriction Act will be introduced immediately' (Gallacher, 1978, p 57). And so it was.

These were extraordinary circumstances, of course. The ability to curtail the supply of munitions was a particularly powerful weapon in wartime. But this weapon was used to great effect. So the Glasgow rent strike represented an extraordinary victory, putting the case for rent controls and for the development of social housing firmly on the agenda for the future – thereby demonstrating what could be achieved, through determined action in the community, backed with solidarity in the workplace.

The shortage of housing also triggered further community action following the Second World War. The housing shortage had been exacerbated by bomb damage, leading desperate families to take action in response. These displaced families *replaced* themselves by occupying empty army camps. By the autumn of 1946 the movement had spread, with organised squatting in empty housing too. Blocks of luxury flats were occupied by hundreds of squatters in London, for example.

Nervous that 'a mass movement of lawless rage against the housing shortage could have swept through many cities [as] people were taking the law into their own hands – the government moved to evict the squatters' (Branson, 1984, p 10). After some discussion, the squatters eventually agreed to leave voluntarily, having first negotiated that they would be rehoused by the relevant local authority (the then London County Council).

Although the squats in question were abandoned, the squatters had held together as a group, and important gains were eventually achieved. The government of the day directed that all requisitioned property that was not required for official purposes should be made available for housing. And the need for more genuinely affordable housing was more firmly on the agenda, as part of the postwar development of the welfare state.

The third example also comes from London, the St Pancras rent strike of 1960. Here, too, as in Glasgow in 1917, community-based resistance was triggered by the demand for rent rises, this time from a Tory local authority rather than from private landlords. The tenants viewed these rent increases as unfair and divisive (because the increases were to vary for different households). But rather than allow themselves to be divided by such mechanisms, the tenants decided to make a stand.

Two of the leaders, Don Cook and Arthur Rowe, agreed to lead this resistance, putting themselves and their families at risk of eviction by refusing to pay the rent increase. With massive community support, marshalled in solidarity to defend them, they barricaded themselves in, to resist eviction. The tenants set up a ship's bell as a warning system, to alert them to action when the bailiffs and the police were on their way. And so the tenants waited, ready to respond.

Eventually the bailiffs did succeed in making an entry. They forced their way in via a neighbouring flat, and then drilled into Don Cook's flat through the roof, so as to avoid having to run the gauntlet of the tenants marshalled outside. After the evictions had taken place there was a mass march down to the Town Hall in protest, with building workers and dockers joining the demonstration in solidarity.

Activists remembered these events in heroic terms, subsequently recounting the story as a folk legend of community resistance. A folk song by Ewan MacColl and Peggy Seeger, entitled 'Hey Ho! Cook and Rowe!' was published celebrating the tenants' struggle – concluding, somewhat optimistically, with the call for 'all you tenants, (to) settle in, Keep up the fight, you're bound to win' (MacColl and Seeger, 1963, p 25). I remember the legendary quality of these events myself, when I became involved in housing issues in the area, and first heard the story, some 10 years later, in the 1970s. Many of those who had been involved in the events around the St Pancras rent strike were still actively involved in the community at that time.

In a community radio programme, recorded some 50 years after these events, housing activists came together to reflect on these past struggles. Overall, they agreed, the St Pancras rent strike had been an extraordinary struggle, "What a day!"

Despite the evictions, they recalled "all sorts of good outcomes." At the next local election, the Tories on the council had been soundly defeated, they explained. Although the rent increases were not reversed, there were no further increases from the incoming council. And the effects began to diminish over time, as a result of inflation. In any case, people were earning better wages by this time, enabling them to afford the previous rent increases more easily.

Activists also reflected that councillors and local authority officers "treated tenants very differently" as a result of these events. The community had "made a stand". They had demanded to be treated with respect and consideration – and they felt that they had achieved this.

For Edie Cook, Don Cook's widow, the memories were more complex. She described how the bailiffs had "frightened the life out of you". She recounted her feelings as she had watched them hurling her family's furniture over the balcony, completely wrecking everything in the process. And that had just been the beginning of the effects of the eviction. After this the family had moved in with her mother. It was several years before they had eventually succeeded in getting a home of their own again. But despite the effects on her family, Edie Cook was still strongly positive about the St Pancras rent strike. She re-affirmed her support for her husband in making this stand, despite knowing the risks involved. The community had taken a stand and this had made "ordinary people who were never politically minded think more", as they reflected on their experiences.

This point was reiterated by Edie Cook's daughter. She had been too young at the time to remember the events in question (and had been at her grandmother's home for safety, when the family's eviction had actually taken place). But she had grown up with the legend of the St Pancras rent strike. This had shaped her own politics, she explained. She was immensely proud of her father for the stand that he had taken, just as she was immensely proud of her mother for her courage in supporting him. (A recording of this interview with Edie Cook, her daughter and another housing activist can be found at http://canstream. co.uk/camden/index.php?id=205)

Although these three stories differ, they do seem to share a number of common strands. In each case, the community in question developed their own response to rising rents and a shortage of genuinely affordable alternatives. Each community demonstrated determination and courage in the pursuit of their strategies of resistance, strategies that entailed their own risks of displacement via eviction procedures. Each was strengthened by practical expressions of solidarity. Each benefited from having effective leadership, including leadership from members of progressive political organisations. And each raised questions about the extent to which the state – whether at national or local levels – or both – could be persuaded to intervene to protect people from displacement as the result of market forces. Activists reflected on the lessons to be shared and the lessons to be passed on for the future.

More recent times

Evictions are still all too frequent, and increasingly so in recent times. In 2015 some 170 people a day were being evicted from their homes in England and Wales, according to the Ministry of Justice's figures, with a total of 42,728 households in rented accommodation being evicted by bailiffs that year, the highest number since records began.

Typically (although not always, of course) these evictions had been due to rent arrears.

Rent arrears have constituted an increasing problem in the context of the current housing crisis. And this has been exacerbated by government 'welfare reforms', cutting benefits, including housing benefits, effectively reducing tenants' abilities to pay. Given the shortage of genuinely affordable housing, the result has been that tenants have been struggling to find cheaper alternatives. So, 'it's boom time for bailiffs, while more poor tenants are turfed out', commentators have argued (Foster, 2016, p 37).

While tenants have been at the sharp end, facing the immediate impact of property market processes, the threat of eviction has been looming over a range of voluntary and community sector organisations and groups too. This is another part of the story, having an impact on services and potentially undermining community-based resources for the future, increasing instability as organisations have found themselves forced to move, again and again, in response to rising office rents.

Chapter Two has already summarised the underlying causes of the housing crisis, together with the reasons why this has been experienced so acutely in London. The growth of the financial sector has been a significant factor, as highly paid professionals have been competing for housing in London's increasingly globalised property market, while the supply of genuinely affordable social housing has been shrinking. The combined effects, with rapid population growth, have been all too evident, with rising housing costs and processes of social cleansing as a result.

The housing crisis has been directly linked to the financialised economy, as the events of 2008 demonstrated only too clearly. Unsustainable mortgage debt in the US provided a trigger for a financial crisis of international proportions. The subsequent effects have been all too evident, with continuing austerity in Britain and elsewhere. The promise of capital gains has been a particular feature of the situation in London, as a global city of capital. Housing offers particular opportunities for investment for capital gains in the London context. This becomes 'Housing for profit, not for people', to turn a popular slogan right around and upside down (Cowley, 1979). The housing in question may not even be occupied, as empty blocks of newly built flats in inner London testify. More than 22,000 homes in London had been left vacant for more than six months, it emerged from a Freedom of Information request in 2016 (although not all of these would have been left empty for these reasons; see Pegg, 2016). Meanwhile hoardings beside development sites close to the City (the financial centre) were announcing the capital gains that could be anticipated, to encourage investors to buy off plan.

There is not the space to explore the impact of financialisation in further detail here. The points to emphasise are simply these. First, housing markets cannot be understood without considering their links with financial markets more generally, markets in which there are winners and losers – the 1% and 99% in popular usage (Weeks, 2014). And second, the housing crisis cannot be understood without reference to the interventions of public policies – and the failures of public policies to protect people from the vagaries of market forces. The state provides tax breaks and effective subsidies for some, but signally fails to provide secure, genuinely affordable homes for others, in the current policy context.

The result has been a crisis of epic proportions. In 2014, Ines Newman and I produced a report for the Centre for Labour and Social Studies, a think tank for left debate and discussion (Mayo and Newman, 2014). This summarised the causes of the national housing crisis, together with the policies that would be needed to tackle this crisis effectively. (This was a pre-election period, so we aimed to inform debate, providing ammunition for those campaigning for progressive alternatives.) In brief we outlined the ways in which displacement had been occurring in recent years from a combination of factors, the decline in building new housing, under previous governments, both Conservative and Labour. The effects of this had been compounded by reductions in the supply of social housing as a result of the sale of 1.78 million council homes in England alone, through the Right to Buy (policies to enable council tenants to buy their homes at a discount). Overall, the stock of council housing had fallen from 32% of the stock in 1979 (before the Right to Buy policy took effect) to just 18% by 2007. While housing associations had been making up some of the shortfall in the supply of social housing, subsequent policy changes had led to increasing rents in this sector, too, with so-called 'affordable' rents for new housing association homes being charged at up to 80% of the market rents in the relevant areas, effectively pricing them way beyond the reach of households on average incomes in high-cost places like inner London.

Meanwhile, the private rented sector had been expanding, with an increase from 2.1 million households in privately rented accommodation in 2001 to 3.6 million in 2012. With the exception of some older tenancies, from 1989 rents in this sector have been unregulated and rising rapidly, along with house prices, especially in areas of acute housing shortage. As a result, young people have been becoming less and less able to afford to buy their own homes, even if they were earning reasonable salaries. It is estimated that by 2020 the proportion of young people in their 20s who would be able to afford a mortgage will halve. By 2025, only one in ten of those under 35 on a modest income will be able to afford to own their own home (Elliott and Osborne, 2016), leaving 'generation rent' with no alternative but to compete for housing in the privately rented sector – where rents are increasingly unaffordable and tenants lack security of tenure. So landlords could put up the rent at the end of a fixed term tenancy, or evict a tenant with just two months' notice – or both – risks that could be exacerbated if tenants had the temerity to complain about poor maintenance and the lack of basic repairs. Some 26% of those accepted as homeless lost their homes as a result of this lack of security in the private rented sector.

The effects were drastic even for those managing to rehouse themselves rather than becoming homeless. In 2016 more than a quarter of families in the privately rented sector – an estimated 400,000 families with children – had been forced to move at least three times in the past five years, according to Shelter. And 65,000 families had been forced to move their children's schools as a result of their last move.

As if the lack of secure and genuinely affordable housing were not problematic enough, in terms of the causes of the housing crisis, the situation was being exacerbated by government welfare 'reforms'. With cutbacks in benefits, claimants were becoming increasingly vulnerable to displacement and dispossession, with the most vulnerable people, including people with disabilities, becoming most seriously at risk. Our paper provided a number of examples to illustrate the combined effects of market forces and public policies, based on research with voluntary and community sector organisations with bases in north London.

> Mr Raines had a serious accident 2 years ago and has been unable to return to work although he hopes to do so in the future. He has a wife and two small sons. The whole family used to live in a studio council flat in London and were severely overcrowded. Camden Council offered to transfer them to a two-bedroom flat owned by a housing association. They decided to take this, a year-and-a-half ago, but the rent is £304 a week while their studio flat rent was only £95 a week. The housing association more than doubled the rent of the flat when it became vacant, moving from a rent that was equivalent to those charged by the council to the so-called "affordable rent", forcing Mr Raines into

arrears and increasing risk of homelessness. (Interview with Ines Newman, quoted in Mayo and Newman, 2014, p 12)

These pressures applied to newcomers to London as well as to longer-established residents, of course.

Amina and her four children had been living in a privately rented flat in the London borough of Camden. In May 2013 her rent rose to £430 a week but her housing allowance [the relevant social welfare benefit] was capped at £330 per week. She fell into arrears as a result and was given notice to quit. (Author's interview with Amina, written up in Mayo and Newman, 2014, p 12)

Displaced from Camden, she moved further out to a cheaper flat, but this had major problems of damp and disrepair. 'Given the insecurity of her tenancy she has struggled to get any progress in relation to these repairs', the report continued.

Meanwhile, the additional travelling that the move entailed was causing problems in terms of time and money. 'Amina is spending £35–£40 per week on travelling at present and gets up at 5am to get to her job in West London', having dropped off her children in school. Even if she had wanted to disrupt her children's education by moving them to different schools, this was not an option as there were insufficient school places in her new area. Unsurprisingly, the report concluded, this situation had been posing major problems for the family (Mayo and Newman, 2014, p 16).

The report concluded that this was indeed a housing crisis, requiring urgent action on a number of fronts – building more genuinely affordable homes, safeguarding the existing social housing stock, protecting private tenants from destitution, rent arrears and eviction, and giving tenants an effective voice to enable them to access their rights for themselves.

Supporting people in their attempts to avoid displacement and dispossession

The SYDRC was providing information, advice and support, for example, alongside its advocacy and campaigning activities more generally (as described in Chapter Three). Refugees and migrants were among the most vulnerable and in need of support, whatever the myths to the contrary. I met with several of those involved and heard their stories of serial displacement.

'Maryam' (not her real name) was initially displaced from Somalia, coming to Britain as a refugee in search of safety and security for herself and her children. Having arrived in Liverpool eight years ago, she had not been able to live in the same place for more than two years. These continual moves had had significant effects on her and her family, as she went on to explain.

The end result had been very damaging. She had missed out on opportunities to take English classes, for instance, and this had affected her chances of obtaining employment. The constant moves had also been extremely disruptive for her three children. They had spent time out of school altogether, even while awaiting the offer of school places, following a move to a new area. Given these difficulties Maryam had tried to keep her children in their existing schools when she next moved, but this had also been extremely problematic, because of the travelling involved. Like Amina, she had been getting up at 5am in order to get everything done and her children ready to start the journey to school in time – a journey that had been involving three separate bus journeys. This had been exhausting for the children as well as for Maryam herself.

The situation had taken its toll on Maryam's health. In addition to the stresses involved in travelling, her previous flat had been on the fourth floor, with no lift, so she had to carry the smallest child, the buggy and shopping up and down four flights of stairs several times a day. As a result she had developed serious problems with her back, problems that were particularly acute each time she moved, when she had to pack up and shift everything by herself.

When she had been living in privately rented accommodation, she had had to struggle with poor housing conditions as well as insecurity. If tenants complained, landlords would move them on, she explained. The continual moves had also been socially isolating. Maryam's extended family members were still in Somalia. Constantly moving, she had found it very difficult to develop her own networks of friendship and support, and this had been depressing, so she was very relieved when, with SYDRC's support, she was eventually rehoused in a council property. She was looking forward to enrolling on an English language course next, with a view to obtaining employment as the next step.

Reflecting on her experiences overall, as a multiply displaced person, she expressed her appreciation of the support that she had been receiving from the Somali community in general, and from SYDRC in particular. This had been crucial, enabling her to settle, and so build a new life for herself and her children.

The housing crisis could affect newcomers, already displaced from their homelands, as well as affecting longer-established residents. There were cross-overs here, as a local housing turned migration activist explained. Ruth explained that her own story also involved histories of displacement. Her four grandparents had all come from Poland, as Jewish refugees fleeing the pogroms – but also in search of more secure livelihoods. This family background had been central to her personal formation and her subsequent engagement with migrants and refugees.

At university Ruth had become active in housing issues and struggles, going on to work with a campaigning organisation that had been formed in response to gentrification, supporting tenants who were at risk of being squeezed out of the area as a result of market forces. She described community campaigning as having been active, imaginative and, to a considerable degree, effective, with support from the relevant local authority, at that time, in the 1970s.

Once she had qualified as a social worker, Ruth had also become involved in mental health issues and campaigns. This was how she had come to focus on working with refugees and asylum-seekers, housing issues and destitution being among their most frequent problems, compounding the mental health effects of the traumas that so many had experienced in the past.

When I checked the draft of this chapter back with Ruth, she responded that there was so much more to be said. Asylum-seekers were having such a tortuous journey, with 'accommodation in racist areas of UK … and rat-infested rooms with doors falling off their hinges. Suicide risk is directly related to living conditions', she pointed out, although her organisation had averted a good share of these, providing the structure needed to support their service users through crises. 'At the worst end of the scale this lack of affordable housing [for young people more generally too] amounts to catastrophic health risks to generations', she concluded, emphasising the risks of suicide and various forms of self-harm (personal communication).

Ruth had given further emphasis to the extent of these problems. But she had also provided examples of some of the extraordinary ways in which people with very little themselves could still offer support to those in even greater need. She had spoken of the amazing generosity that she had come across, both from members of refugees' own communities, and from churches and others in the local community where she still lived and worked as a volunteer. But this was against a background of cuts, affecting voluntary organisations like the one that she had established herself, struggling to support individuals and refugee communities to support each other.

Ruth had concluded with some reflections on the importance of building solidarity, including solidarity between refugees and those facing displacement via market forces in inner London. Refugees really needed this type of solidarity as well as having the immediate need of a roof over their heads, with practical advice and support from voluntary and community-based organisations and groups.

Community resistance campaigns

Tenants and residents were also organising their own campaigns of resistance, as the previous chapter has already illustrated. 'Social housing, not social cleansing' was the banner slogan for New Era tenants in Hoxton, East London, for example, campaigning to keep rents at an affordable level for existing tenants in the 93 homes on the estate. As their petition explained, 'Our estate, the New Era Estate in Hoxton, has a long history of providing affordable housing and has been home to some people for 70 years. It is home to families who have built their lives in this area' (see www.change.org/p/new-era-should-not-become-the-end-of-an-era). 'But the property firm Westbrook Partners have recently bought the estate', the petition continued,

> … and are planning a massive rent hike that will treble what we pay now. We're calling on the firm to ensure long-term affordable rent so that our families aren't forced to be made homeless…. The cost of the forces of change has been paid by individuals and families, who are being forced from the area they were born and grew up in. The approach of profit over people is devastating lives and shredding long standing communities, to such an extent that the Mayor of Hackney, Jules Pipe, has said that the treatment of tenants is unfair and that the proposed rent increases are "tearing the heart out of Hoxton".

As a result of vigorous campaigning (a campaign that included public support from the comedian, Russell Brand) the estate was eventually taken over by a housing charity, Dolphin Living, committed to enabling existing tenants to be able to afford to stay. 'YES!!! WE WON!!!' The tenants announced. 'People power works.'

The new landlord's proposals involved their own challenges, however. Rents were to be linked to tenants' incomes, so the better-off tenants would pay up to double the rents of the poorest on the estate, which was potentially divisive. Unsurprisingly, as Lindsey Garrett, a resident who had played a leading role in the campaign, reflected, the proposal had been contentious. 'A lot of people are saying it is not fair they will be paying more than they were', she said. 'But from where I stand it is hard to argue against it', she concluded, as those with higher incomes could actually afford to pay more, a view that was generally accepted by the majority of people on the estate, it seemed (Booth, 2015).

Others were less optimistic. The director of Generation Rent (a group campaigning for affordable housing) made the following comment: 'It will work until Dolphin runs out of money and then the subsidy will stop.' 'The real test', he continued, 'will be what they do when someone moves out. There will be an incentive, not just for the landlord, but for the tenants to get a higher rent payer in. It is unsustainable' (quoted in Booth, 2015). Bucking market forces might prove more problematic, then?

Despite the challenges, however, at the time of writing, in 2016, New Era was still going strong. With support from Russell Brand, a community cafe, the Trew Era cafe, was opened in 2015, staffed by a professional manager along with local people recovering from various forms of difficulties in their lives. They were all receiving a regular wage: these jobs were described as being 'proper jobs', giving them pride and self-esteem. When I visited the cafe in the summer of 2016, I could see for myself that this was a well-used community hub, meeting people's individual needs as well as providing an established gathering place for the local community.

From 'perfect storm' to 'perfect tsunami'?

As if bucking market forces was not problematic enough, in the contemporary context the prognosis for the future seems even more challenging. The housing crisis is expected to deepen following legislative changes to be implemented via the Housing and Planning Act, passed in 2016.

Taken together, the provisions of this legislation could pose major threats to the very notion of mixed communities. The housing crisis risks being exacerbated as a result, leading to further displacement and social cleansing. Market-driven public policies have been compounding the problems when governments should have been doing the very opposite, housing activists were arguing, campaigning for alternative policies to protect communities from displacement and dispossession.

So activists mobilised to campaign against the proposed changes. The 'Kill the Housing Bill' came together in December 2015 as an alliance of tenants of all tenures, housing workers, MPs, traveller groups (also affected by proposed reductions to permanent sites for travellers), councillors and trade unions, all concerned at the threats that were being posed. As the campaign's briefing paper argued, 'This Bill would be a disaster if implemented. For the huge section of the population struggling to meet their housing needs, this Bill offers nothing. We demand a solution to the housing crisis that ensures that every citizen can access a decent and secure home we can afford. And we need to do it now.' 'Genuinely affordable housing is a necessity for a stable life', the briefing paper continued, arguing that 'the market will not provide it. Subsidy to developers, lenders and private landlords continue while ministers remove investment in sustainable housing for rent' (Kill the Housing Bill, 2015).

There were packed meetings in some town halls and community centres, as I experienced for myself, as well as packed meetings in Parliament, supported by a number of MPs, including the Leader of the Opposition and the Shadow Chancellor.

From the outset, campaigners were clear about the importance of building solidarity, involving those who owned their own homes as well as those who were renting, whatever the tenure. This was about the future of genuinely affordable housing, with opportunities and choices for people's children and grandchildren. And this included emphasising the importance of building solidarity with newcomers. Refugees and migrants were *not* the cause of the housing crisis, it was argued, nor were they being rehoused in preference to long-standing residents, however understandable people's anxieties on these scores were. On the contrary, newcomers were just as affected by the housing crisis, as Amina and Maryam's stories have already illustrated. As it was also pointed out, the Syrian refugees who were to be accommodated in the coming period would not be housed in high-cost areas such as inner London, because the rents there would be far beyond the resources available for their resettlement.

Subsequent chapters return to some of the issues and challenges involved in building solidarity within and between communities alongside social movements more generally. Meanwhile, at the time of writing, campaigning against the Housing and Planning Act was continuing, with activists continuing to mobilise over the plans for implementation, winning significant concessions in the process.

Learning from experience

Reflecting on their experiences, a number of activists referred to the processes of learning that had been involved, emphasising the importance of sharing this learning with others in and between communities. One of the first priorities of the 'Kill the Housing Bill' campaign was precisely this, to ensure that the implications of this Bill were fully understood, so that communities could be mobilised in response to the threats of displacement being posed. Local authorities were encouraged to write to their tenants, for example, following up their letters with local meetings on estates. This would complement the educational activities being undertaken by tenants and residents' organisations and groups themselves.

While providing such specific information was essential, this was not the only aspect of people's learning. People could and did also learn wider lessons from their experiences. As Edie Cook commented, looking back on the experiences of those who had taken a stand in the St Pancras rent strike, this had made "ordinary people who were never politically minded think more" as they reflected on their experiences – a point reiterated by her daughter and other activists. People had made a stand, and this made a difference to their thinking for the longer term.

There were also examples of people taking their learning with them when they moved from one context to another. Ruth had imbibed her understanding of newcomers' experiences from her own family background. She took this with her, along with her understanding of the problems of housing, homelessness and destitution, when she became active, setting up a project to support migrants and refugees, enabling them to support each other more effectively.

While community activists could and did learn from their own experiences, as other studies have similarly demonstrated (Foley, 1999; Mayo et al, 2013), this was not to the exclusion of learning from those with professional expertise. This type of learning emerged in the previous chapter, for example, as with the case of the Heygate Estate. When the developers had argued that their plans for redeveloping the estate would be unviable unless the proportion of social housing was to be reduced, expert knowledge had been required in order to present the counter arguments effectively. The group had benefited from legal expertise, along with other forms of specialist knowledge and experience, in order to be able to do this. Important lessons had been learned and subsequently shared with others as a result. These lessons had included knowledge about the processes of making planning applications, about making Freedom of Information requests and about local authority processes and procedures more generally. The role of experts had been vitally important – with experts on tap supporting but not dominating the communities in question, as already argued. Chapter Three has provided similar instances, including examples from India, illustrating the scope for professionals to provide communities with expertise, but without taking their campaigns over in the process.

Wider theoretical implications? Reflecting on varying experiences

So how might such learning relate to learning about wider debates, based on differing theoretical perspectives on migration and displacement more generally? How did communities' experiences relate to the neoliberal view that free markets provide the most effective way to promote development, to the ultimate benefit of all concerned? Hardly the experiences of those displaced by market forces.

Or were communities' experiences more consistent with a historical-structuralist critique, illustrating some of the ways in which market forces may indeed produce winners but also losers – those who have been experiencing insecurity and displacement from the effects of market forces? Legacies of the past – including legacies of colonialism – also have continuing relevance from a historical-structuralist perspective, shaping patterns of inequality, conflict and displacement in the context of neoliberal globalisation.

As previous chapters have also pointed out, financialisation has been a defining feature of neoliberal globalisation, with effects that have been particularly – but by no means solely – evident in world cities such as London. In summary, the point to emphasise is simply this. Market forces have been key drivers for better, as their advocates would argue, or indeed for worse, as their critics maintain. Among the critics, Sassen (2014) has already been quoted among the critics. She has identified a number of common underlying strands running through varying types of expulsions, exemplifying different aspects of what she describes as 'brutality and complexity in the global economy' . This complexity, she argues, makes it hard to trace lines of responsibility for the displacements, evictions and eradications that contemporary capitalism produces, and equally hard for those who benefit to feel responsible for its depredations.

Sassen starts from the emergence of 'new logics of *expulsion*' (Sassen, 2014, p 1, emphasis in original) over the past two decades, with 'a sharp growth in the number of people, enterprises, and places expelled from the core social and economic orders of our time.' She includes here the expulsion of low-income and unemployed workers from government welfare benefits, along with refugees displaced by violence, farmers displaced by foreign investors in the global South, and those displaced by environmental degradation – not to forget those displaced as the result of austerity policies, in Greece and elsewhere, or those evicted from their homes as a result of mortgage foreclosures in the US and elsewhere. There are common factors involved in these different forms of expulsion, she argues, leading to increasing inequalities within as well as between countries internationally. The global city is one of the sites where these factors come together, in her view. But the underlying market forces that give rise to these expulsions are comparable, wherever they are taking place.

Financialisation processes are central to Sassen's argument, processes that have been key to the development of global cities. As she goes on to explain, increasing financialisation has been central to the housing crisis. Financial experts have developed extremely sophisticated instruments, enabling profits to be made from 'transforming what might look like a traditional mortgage into part of a speculative instrument to be sold and bought in speculative markets' (Sassen, 2014, p 122). Without going into detail as to the complex ways in which such financial instruments were being developed, the end result was that modest households found themselves in high-risk situations, 'opening up the world of lower-middle-income households to the high circuits of finance' (Sassen, 2014, p 123). Financiers could make profits as a result, while the households in question bore the risks when the subprime mortgage market collapsed in 2008, with catastrophic effects for millions of people on modest incomes. This was but one example of the workings of financialisation, illustrating the complexity of the processes involved, together with the effects in terms of growing extremes of wealth and poverty. 'We now know that the profits secured by the richer segments of society do not "trickle down"', she reflected; rather the reverse. And the more financialised an economy, the more vulnerable to crisis and the greater the risks, particularly for the poorest and most vulnerable in society.

While the processes of financialisation were complex, making it more and more difficult to trace the lines of responsibility, Sassen continued, the economic, social and environmental impacts have been only too evident. But far from being prepared to address these impacts, through effective government actions, governments, central bankers and international organisations have argued for less public intervention and less public spending, to reduce government debts. This was the rationale behind the austerity programme imposed on

Greece, exemplifying austerity programmes that could be conceived, in her view, as 'a weakening and degrading of the project of the liberal welfare state, broadly understood' (Sassen, 2014, p 218).

Whatever their shortcomings, from Sassen's perspective, welfare states could, in principle, secure a measure of socioeconomic redistribution. There was at least some evidence of efforts to promote social inclusion, enabling the disadvantaged to fight for their rights and for social justice. But the logic of what was happening in the contemporary context was the reverse, she concluded, with environmental degradation and expulsions affecting more and more people in varying contexts across the globe.

Welfare states have been classified according to different models, as these have been developed in varying contexts over time. Esping-Andersen's typology, as set out in *The three worlds of welfare capitalism* (Esping-Andersen, 1990), has particular relevance here, providing a framework for considering Sassen's conclusions about welfare states more generally. According to Esping-Andersen, welfare states can be defined according to the degree of decommodification that they involve. In other words, Esping-Andersen was concerned to explore the extent to which states did, or did not, intervene in markets in order to promote welfare. At one end of the spectrum, social democratic states, such as particular Scandinavian states at the time that he was writing, exemplified the most significant degrees of intervention and public spending on welfare. At the other end of the spectrum, in contrast, the US exemplified the type with the least decommodification, most committed to the provision of welfare via the private sector. Welfare states could, of course, develop and change over time though. This was the case with Britain that had been relatively social democratic in the postwar period, in Esping-Andersen's view. But Britain had been moving closer towards the least decommodified category in more recent times, he had concluded.

Esping-Andersen's approach has been subjected to various criticisms, including its lack of focus on the ways in which states address – or fail to address – equal opportunities issues along with the ways in which they address – or fail to address – issues of participation and empowerment (Deakin, 1993). But the focus on decommodification has particular relevance still in the context of neoliberal globalisation. As Harvey and others have previously argued (Harvey, 2010; Fox Piven and Minnite, 2015), neoliberalism had been attempting to unfetter capitalism from the constraints imposed by the inroads of democratic politics over the past three decades.

Neoliberalism has not, of course, implied that states should refrain from any form of public intervention at all. On the contrary, they have been intervening in a number of ways, with a particular focus on facilitating market mechanisms, bailing out banks, for example. As Fox Piven and Minnite have pointed out, states such as the US 'craft policies to mesh more closely with market incentives and disincentives' (Fox Piven and Minnite, 2015, p 145), policies that result in increasing poverty and inequality along with increasing dispossession and displacement. Populist movements and politicians of the radical right may have very different views on the role of the state, as Chapter Two has already outlined, but these are essentially criticisms from *within* rather than *against* the framework of dominant market forces more generally. While fully recognising the impact of market–driven policies, in contrast, Fox Piven and Minnite conclude by emphasising the importance of understanding the potential impact of poor people's movements, with 'disruption from below'. Despite the obstacles, the politics of the poor could still lead to remarkable achievements, in their view.

People still have agency, despite the underlying constraints, as will be suggested in more detail in the following chapter. And this applies to communities and social movements, coming together in response to the challenges of dispossession and dispersal. As Farnsworth and Irving have gone on to point out, governments and international agencies also make choices, including choices to pursue austerity policies. Austerity can be characterised as 'a political response to crisis and prevailing economic conditions' (Farnsworth and Irving, 2015, p 14), while recognising that:

> … as a procession of theorists from Marx to Poulantzas (1972) to Charles Lindblom (1977) would remind us, it is important not to forget in the analysis of political agency the very real structural constraints faced by governments from hostile economic environments, even if those environments are of their own making. (Farnsworth and Irving, 2015, p 14)

Austerity policies have not simply related to economic choices and constraints, however. Austerity policies were going way beyond the cuts in Farnsworth and Irving's view, 'reconfiguring and transforming welfare states and, in the process, undermining welfare state institutions and structures and the social relations they support' (Farnsworth and Irving, 2015, p 15). Austerity policies may not work, in terms of promoting economic growth, they added, but they may certainly work in terms of undermining solidarity and cohesion, constituting 'a powerful counterforce to the threat of a more progressive social democratic welfare state' (Farnsworth and Irving, 2015, p 35), 'undermining political legitimacy and encouraging electorates across Europe and beyond to look to more radical alternatives' (Farnsworth and Irving, 2015, p 38), whether of the radical left or indeed of the radical right.

This last point about the resurgence of the radical right has particular significance in the contemporary context. Political legitimacy has been undermined, as neoliberal austerity policies have been having an impact in increasingly unequal ways across the globe. And people's opinions have been shifting accordingly, whether to the further right or the further left of the political spectrum. There is not the space here to explore these arguments in further detail. The point to emphasise is simply this, that there are choices to be made, whether for better, or indeed for worse, as the following chapter goes on to explore.

SIX

Choices and constraints

As the previous chapter has already argued, people do have agency and they can and do make choices – for better or indeed for worse. How far do people make such choices freely, however, rather than having their 'choices' effectively determined by structural constraints? And how might individuals' rights to choose need to take account of wider social interests and needs? These have constituted questions for philosophers over past centuries, as well as providing questions for social scientists to debate in more contemporary contexts.

Having summarised these wider debates, this chapter moves on to focus on the implications. How might these debates apply to the particular experiences and choices available – or not available – to migrants, refugees and asylum-seekers more specifically? How might they relate to the experiences of those migrating in response to market forces, moving in search of livelihoods elsewhere? And what might these debates imply for policy-making processes within structures of governance?

The chapter concludes by focusing on some of the ways in which people and communities can be supported, to enable them to exercise their agency to the maximum effect. Community education can contribute here, facilitating learning, including learning from people's experiences of collective engagement. As the previous chapter has already pointed out, people can and do learn from each other. And this learning can be enhanced by those with particular areas of expertise, including those with expertise in using community arts as tools to facilitate collective learning, the arts being particularly effective when it comes to addressing people's emotions (Boal, 1979, 1995; Clover and Sandford, 2013; Rooke, 2013; Tiller, 2013).

Free will or determinism?

As the *Cambridge dictionary of philosophy* explains, 'For those who contrast "free" with "determined", a central question is whether humans are free in what they do or determined by external events beyond their control' (Kapitan, 1995, p 280). Philosophers continue to debate this question, together with its potential implications. Might there be limits to the desirability of unbridled freedom, even if this were actually possible in practice?

As John Gray's enquiry into human freedom points out, there are ethical dilemmas to be addressed when humans attempt to master total control (Gray, 2015). Such attempts at mastery can lead to violence, in Gray's view, including blood-letting against minorities – 'Jews, gay people, immigrants and others who may seem different' (Gray, 2015, p 81). Modern individualism has its downside, he suggests, the accompanying freedoms being achieved at the expense of social solidarity and social cohesion. The rich may succeed in contriving such individual freedoms for themselves, he concludes. But this can lead to fears of envy and popular discontent from the masses, fears that may result in increasing surveillance and loss of privacy for the rest. These philosophical deliberations have significant implications for public policy considerations, including questions concerning the extent to which state interventions can be justified (Sen, 1992; Sandel, 1998; Nussbaum, 2003), debates that Chapter Two and the previous chapter have already set out, in outline.

Agency versus structure?

Social scientists have also been concerned to explore the issue of human agency from varying perspectives, identifying the origins of these debates within the history of the development of sociology as a discipline (Giddens, 1989). For example, founding father Émile Durkheim's study of suicide made the case for the fundamental significance of social factors as explanations for such an apparently personal choice as the decision to take one's own life. While suicide might appear to be caused by extreme personal unhappiness, in Durkheim's view, suicide rates were actually 'social facts', showing regular patterns that varied from one society to another, variations that could be explained sociologically (Durkheim, 1952). Structure was winning out here, according to Durkheim, relegating the scope for human agency to the side lines of sociological enquiry – an approach that has been the subject of much subsequent debate.

Although Marx developed a very different theoretical approach to the study of society, he, too, emphasised the significance of structural factors, focusing on class formations and class conflicts as these were developing in capitalist societies. History could be understood in terms of these structural conflicts, rooted in the relations of production that predominated within particular social contexts (Marx, 1968).

Critics have argued with this for being too deterministic as an approach, allowing too little scope for human agency, debates that have continued through to more recent times (Poulantzas, 1972). But Marx himself firmly rejected overly determinist interpretations of his work. 'Men make their own history', Marx pointed out 'but they do not make it as they please; they do not make it under self-selected circumstances, but under circumstances existing already, given and transmitted from the past' (Marx, 1968, p 98), going on to refer to the influence of past ideas rather than simply focusing on economic factors as examples of the types of structural constraints that he had in mind.

The role of ideas has been a continuing theme within Marxist debates, in fact. How far do the ideas that are predominant, within particular societies, reflect the underlying interests of the most powerful? Take the view, for example, that, for the economy to recover, following the financial crisis of 2008, austerity policies would have to be endured. Such views may have appeared to be common sense at the time, but they have actually been contentious, as already argued, austerity being a political choice rather than an economic necessity (Farnsworth and Irving, 2015). So ideas can be powerful weapons, justifying – or alternatively, challenging – the status quo (Gramsci, 1986), key elements within wider struggles for social justice and equalities. People's ideas may be influenced by their social contexts (Bourdieu, 2003), but they may also be challenged and changed, opening up new possibilities for social action in the process.

Without going into further detail here, the point to emphasise is simply this, that, like philosophers, social scientists and political economists have been similarly concerned to explore the balances to be struck – how to take account of the varying types of structural explanations, on the one hand, without losing sight of explanations that focus on human agency and the construction of meanings, on the other. And social scientists have been concerned to explore the ways in which these factors interact, as people's social contexts have an impact on their consciousness, without mechanistically determining their responses, as social actors with agency rather than as marionettes or puppets on strings (Bourdieu, 2003; Gray, 2015).

These debates are being taken forward in varying ways in the current context. Marxists have been exploring the impacts of the structural changes that have been associated with neoliberal globalisation and increasing financialisation, as previous chapters have already suggested (Lapavitsas, 2013; Sassen, 2014). And neoliberals have been taking very different positions, emphasising the ways in which individuals have agency, taking decisions as rational actors in the pursuit of their own interests, as previous chapters have also suggested.

Meanwhile, in contrast, social scientists who have been drawing on psychosocial perspectives have been questioning the very notion of human beings as wholly rational individuals, unaffected by their emotions as they make supposedly considered choices, each in pursuit of his or her self-interest. On the contrary, from a psychosocial perspective, people's choices need to be understood in ways that take account of the world of emotions, including subconscious emotions, as the personal interacts with the social and the political, in people's lived experiences (Hoggett, 2000). Psychosocial approaches have particular relevance in relation to stories of displacement, stories that have been laden with emotional implications, both positively and more negatively, evoking feelings of compassion and solidarity alongside feelings of hatred and fear.

For example, W.G. Sebald's *The emigrants* documents the lives of four Jewish emigrants in the 20th century. As one of these four, Ferber, tells the story of his life, he explains how he was affected by learning of his parents' deportations in 1941 under the Nazi regime. Ferber himself had managed to reach England as a child, taking refuge with his uncle. He was physically safe, if emotionally troubled, as a result. 'I took steps, consciously or unconsciously, to keep at bay thoughts of my parents' sufferings and of my own misfortune', he explained, adding that he sometimes succeeded 'in maintaining a certain equability by my self-imposed seclusion.' But still, he continued, 'the fact is that that tragedy in my youth struck such deep roots within me that it later shot up again, put forth evil flowers, and spread the poisonous canopy over me which has kept me so much in the shade and dark in recent years' (Sebald, 1997, p 191).

Ferber had planned to follow his uncle to New York when his uncle left for a new life there, in 1942. 'But, when the time came' (having finished his last year of schooling in England), Ferber explained, 'I did not want to be reminded of my origins by anything or anyone, so instead of going to New York, into the care of my uncle, I decided to move to Manchester on my own' (Sebald, 1997, p 191). 'I imagined I could begin a new life from scratch' – except that 'Manchester reminded me of everything I was trying to forget' (Sebald, 1997, p 191). Manchester was an immigrant city and 'the immigrants were chiefly Germans and Jews' (Sebald, 1997, p 191). And so, he continued, 'although I had intended to move in the opposite direction, when I arrived in Manchester I had come home, in a sense' (Sebald, 1997, p 192).

The role of emotions emerges only too clearly, then, when it comes to trying to make sense of people's choices, including our own behaviours as well as the behaviours of others.

So how might such debates about agency and structure and the limits of rational actor theories apply to the experiences of individuals and communities facing threats of displacement and dispossession more generally? And how might people be supported, to enable them to maximise the effects of their actions, making informed choices while taking account of wider constraints? But first a brief digression, to consider the situations of those who have been affected by structural constraints in very different ways – ways in which structural constraints have been confining rather than displacing them, all too literally keeping them in their place.

Resisting being kept in one's place?

As Harvey and others have already pointed out, displacement is far from being the only threat for poor communities. 'Low income populations, usually lacking the means to overcome and hence command space, find themselves for the most part trapped in space' (Harvey, 1989, p 265). People may be unable to afford to move from impoverished and polluted environments, where public services, such as education, housing, health and social care tend to be provided least effectively. And these disadvantages may be compounded even further, given the social stigma so often attached to such neighbourhoods (postcodes from which employers decline to recruit their staff). The women portrayed in Mckenzie's study of St Ann's, Nottingham, for example, were only too well aware of being looked down on like this. As one of them explained, 'they think everyone around here is gangsters' (quoted in Mckenzie, 2015, p 65). Living in St Ann's was part of their problem, although this had its upside too. St Ann's provided them with a sense of community, offering safety from class prejudice and social stigma (Mckenzie, 2015).

Minority communities may also be effectively confined within ghettos, whether by deliberate design, or as the result of poverty and inequality, exacerbated by popular prejudices and fears of racist violence. Hoque's study of third-generation Bangladeshi people from East London provides just such an example. Following a racist murder in East London in 1993, some people from minority backgrounds were described as having become prisoners in the own homes, in a climate of fear (Hoque, 2015).

Although this was a particularly threatening situation, the fears that this racist murder raised compounded existing feelings of anxiety.

The young Bangladeshi people that Hoque interviewed reflected these emotions of anxiety and exclusion, describing themselves as feeling like 'outcast(s)' and 'stranger(s)' (quoted in Hoque, 2015, p 78). Akbar's memories of clashes between British National Front followers and Bangladeshi people in the 1990s led him to see white people as separate from 'us', for example, just as Sanjida's experiences of direct racism caused similarly painful feelings of displacement, rejection and fear. 'We would constantly hear things such as "Go back to your own country, you don't belong here"', leading her to question 'Why did we come here in the first place? Where do we actually belong if we don't belong here? We used to be scared to come out of our own house even to go to the local shops' (quoted in Hoque, 2015, p 79).

The fear of encountering homophobic violence may have similarly confining effects for lesbian, gay, bi-sexual and transvestite communities. And people with disabilities may be effectively imprisoned in their homes, too. This may be due to fear of discrimination and abuse. Or because they lack the resources to facilitate their mobility. Or both, in a climate of austerity cuts, accompanied by the increasing vilification of anyone suspected of welfare 'scrounging'.

Parallel arguments have also been applied to women's circumstances. As Fiona Williams and others have pointed out, women may be trapped in the locality of their communities, place-bound and tied by a range of factors arising from their situations as women, including ties arising from their domestic and family responsibilities (Williams, 1989; Massey, 1994). And women may be kept in their place by the fear of violence outside.

A particularly striking example, illustrating ways in which women and girls are being kept in their place, emerges from participatory research in India. Poverty and inequality feature as causal factors here, but so, too, do more ideological and emotional factors, negative attitudes and prejudices that have an impact on the lives of women and girls, restricting their mobility, effectively confining them within the domestic sphere.

The Kadam Badhate Chalo (KBC) project was launched in 2013 by PRIA, the Indian-based NGO introduced in Chapter Four. I was privileged to be directly involved with this particular PRIA project, engaging with the development of KBC's evaluation strategy in 2016.

The origins of KBC relate back to the horrific rape of a young woman in Delhi in December 2012, a case that led to widespread publicity, as the victim was able to testify against her attackers before she died of her injuries, 13 days later. In response, the KBC project set out to work with young people (boys as well as girls), to challenge violence against women and girls, young people being identified as potentially key change makers, the hope for the future. In line with PRIA's approach more generally, the emphasis was participatory, supporting young people to enable them to take the lead in changing attitudes within their communities, promoting institutional accountability and developing multi-stakeholder coalitions in the process.

For the purposes of this particular chapter, the most relevant aspect of KBC's initiatives relates to their participatory mapping exercises. Separately, girls and boys produced maps of their villages (or their wards, in urban areas), marking different areas according to how safe – or unsafe – they felt. The safest places were marked with smiley stickers ☺, the least safe with scowling stickers ☹, with neutral-looking stickers ☺ for the places that were deemed to be in between, neither safe nor particularly unsafe. The two groups then compared their maps before sharing the findings more widely with their families and communities, identifying action points such as the need for improved street lighting and security cameras in particularly unsafe places.

Perhaps unsurprisingly, the girls' maps were very different from the boys' maps, although these differences did sometimes cause some surprise to the young people themselves. During one of my first visits, in Jaipur, I heard this directly from a group of the young people who had been involved. The boys had been shocked to find that there were so few places where the girls felt safe at all, they told me. Home seemed to be almost the only safe place, in fact (despite domestic realities such as the risks of domestic violence and dowry-related violence, just to mention two of the most obvious hazards in the home for women and girls).

So many women and girls were living such circumscribed lives as a result, effectively kept in their places by their only too understandable fears of varying forms of violence. And these fears were being continually re-enforced by patriarchal attitudes – blaming girls for provoking problems by wearing tight clothes, or being too mouthy, for instance, views that are also being expressed in many contexts elsewhere.

As the report on KBC's progress in Jaipur went on to explain, further discussion led to widespread recognition that violence against women and girls occurs irrespective of their clothing or audacity, demonstrating the possibility of shifting attitudes, working towards building some shared responsibility for social change (see http://pria.org).

If structural disadvantages were contributing towards keeping some people *in their place*, so were attitudes and behaviours, factors that could also be challenged and changed. Individuals and communities could and did make choices. And some changes could be observable, even within the context of wider structural constraints, as the KBC projects were demonstrating.

Agency and/or structure and displacement

This takes the discussion back to considering the varying explanations for people's *displacement* as set out in Chapter Two. Differing theoretical approaches have offered competing perspectives here, with neoliberal approaches emphasising the significance of each individual's agency as a rational actor, weighing up the different factors involved and then making decisions for the future, taking account of his or her best interests. Meanwhile, in contrast, historical-structural theorists were focusing on the wider contexts as these had been developing in particular places over time, shaping the constraints that were having an impact on people's choices, both individually and collectively, in their communities (Castles et al, 2014).

There are potential implications, too, when it comes to defining the distinctions between refugees and migrants more generally. As Chapter Two has already outlined, the UNHCR definition distinguishes between migrants 'who choose to move not because of a direct threat of persecution or death' (the factors involved in refugees' decisions to leave) but 'mainly to improve their lives by finding work, or in some cases education, family reunion, or other reasons' (UNHCR, 2015). Refugees are to be distinguished, in contrast, by the direct threats of persecutions or death that they face. So, in popular discourse, refugees can be portrayed as victims, in need of sanctuary, while migrants can be portrayed in far more problematic terms.

Refugees have certainly written of their lack of choice when they found themselves forced to flee from their homelands. Novelist and playwright Gillian Slovo expressed this clearly, when she reflected on her own experiences. It had been her 12th birthday when she arrived with her family, both her parents having had to leave South Africa because of their respective roles as prominent anti-apartheid campaigners (Slovo, 2016). When her mother, the journalist Ruth First, had been released from prison, following 117 days' detention in solitary confinement, she had fled to Britain with her family, in search of asylum, in 1964.

As Gillian Slovo reflected, because her parents were well-known anti-apartheid activists, 'when we arrived at Heathrow, we didn't have to do what most refugees do, which is to declare ourselves', their need for asylum being all too evident. As she went on to add, 'I wasn't what most people think of when they imagine a refugee – I'm white, I speak English, I'm well-educated, I arrived on an aeroplane. I didn't have to risk my life in a flimsy boat.'She was struck by how lucky she was, in fact, comparing the circumstances of her arrival with those of more recent refugees attempting to come to Europe from war zones. 'But it's important to remember', she concluded, 'that becoming a refugee is not a choice. It is something that can happen to anyone. It happened to me' (Slovo, 2016, p 9).

The Kenyan writer, Ngugi wa Thiong'o, wrote about his experiences of exile in similar vein. 'I never chose exile; it was forced on me', he reflected, looking back on his flight from the threat of being 'eliminated' under the Moi dictatorship in 1982. In London for a book launch, he had been planning to return home when he was warned of the impending threat to his liberty, if not his life. So he decided not to risk going back. But his feelings were complex. He continued to hope to return, his suitcase remaining still packed and ready to go, in anticipation, just in case (Ngugi wa Thiong'o, 2015).

'Exile is more than separation' he continued. 'It is longing for home, exaggerating its virtues with every encounter with inconvenience.' Having had little, if any, effective choice about his decision not to return, he remained emotionally engaged by the pull of home. As he went on to explain, as a 10-year-old child he had been moved by the love and solidarity that he had seen among a group of Kenyan prisoners who were passing by, caged in a lorry in a convoy of vehicles. They were singing, despite their hardships, as they were being forcibly relocated from their lands to make room for white settlers. This was an image, Ngugi explained, 'that captured vividly the ideals of mutual care and collective hope in the anti-colonial resistance' (Ngugi wa Thiong'o, 2015).

The pull of home continued for Ngugi. He did eventually return, following the electoral defeat of the Moi dictatorship in 2003, but yet again, as on previous returns, he was forced to flee for his life, he and his wife having been brutally attacked by four armed gunmen, 11 days after their arrival in Kenya. Once again he had little, if any, effective choice but to leave.

Ngugi reflected on this cycle of departures and returns, seeing this as central to his writing. He was clinging on to the 'unfulfilled dream the caged men and women once sang about' (Ngugi wa Thiong'o, 2015), he explained. It was through their eyes that he had looked at the performance of the various postcolonial governments in Kenya and found them wanting. 'One day I will unpack the suitcase in the mind', he concluded, to write about America and Europe, rather than continuing to focus on his native Kenya. 'But I hope I will still find inspiration from those caged men and women whose melody of defiance embodies the dreams of all those who dream to change the world for the empowerment of the least among us' (Ngugi wa Thiong'o, 2015).

Ngugi wa Thiong'o had little if any choice, then, except to become a refugee. And yet he had felt compelled to keep returning, both in person and in his writings, because of the emotional pull of home.

Other writers have expressed similarly mixed feelings about becoming refugees, including the German novelist, Thomas Mann. He first went into exile, fleeing Germany in 1933, horrified by the Nazis and deeply shaken by the lack of effective opposition among the German population more generally. But despite these feelings about his homeland, when he subsequently took refuge in the US in 1938, he famously declared that, 'Where I am, there is Germany', becoming a cultural leader among German exiles, including musicians as well as writers. He was a generous supporter of German refugees, including many Jewish refugees, describing his house as having become 'a rescue bureau for people in danger ... people crying for help, people going under' (quoted in Meyers, 2012).

Reflecting on Thomas Mann's time as a refugee in America, Meyers has pointed out that, unlike the Jewish writers who had been forced out of Germany, Mann could, if he had so wished, stayed put and profitably collaborated with the Nazis, as indeed others did (Meyers, 2012). But he hated everything that Hitler stood for, and this was why he left. So how far might Thomas Mann's decision to leave be described as a matter of 'choice'? Once he had spoken out, the options must have seemed somewhat limited, with even less in the way of options, perhaps, once his books had been burnt in Germany. But could he have chosen not to speak out in the first place?

Can refugees actually be distinguished from migrants so clearly, in practice? The UNHCR definition focuses specifically on forced displacement. The structural factors that have an impact on migrants' decisions to move are excluded from consideration, factors such as poverty and/or diminishing opportunities for sustainable livelihoods – whether as the result of drought and famine, for instance, or as the result of economic constraints.

The case for having a clear definition, providing guidelines for sorting out who is – and who is not – a refugee is understandable, of course, from governments' perspectives, although even these guidelines may be interpreted by differing governments and then acted on in varying ways. The realities of people's circumstances and choices – or lack of choices – as migrants would seem more complex, however.Colm Toibin's novel *Brooklyn*, now also a major motion picture, depicts this complexity through the story of a young Irish woman, Eilis Lacey, who emigrates to Brooklyn, New York in the 1950s. When the novel opens Eilis is offered a part-time job, half a day a week on Sundays, serving in a shop in her native Ireland. But this isn't what she needs. She takes the job, but as she goes on to tell her mother when she gets home, 'I'm just there until something turns up' (Toibin, 2009, p 11). A proper job. This is what her mother says that she is praying for her, every day.

And something does turn up in the form of Father Flood, a priest on a visit from the US. 'In the United States', he explains, 'there would be plenty of work for someone like you and with good pay' (Toibin, 2009, p 22). Is this a no brainer, or not? Whatever the opportunities across the ocean, her mother points out, America is very far away. 'Parts of Brooklyn are just like Ireland', Father Flood reassures her. 'They're full of Irish' (Toibin, 2009, p 23). And so, in the silence that ensues, Eilis comes to understand that it has somehow been tacitly arranged that she will go to the US, the land of opportunity, where people can become rich.

Reflecting on growing up in this part of Ireland himself, Colm Toibin describes his own view of the emigrants who came back to visit from America at this time as being full of glamour. 'In America, they made clear, you could become a millionaire' (Toibin, 2009, p 258). No one who goes to America misses home, it was said, although Eilis herself wonders if that could actually be entirely true.

Eilis's story mirrors that of so many migrants at that time. Although her family was not actually on the breadline, economic opportunities were strictly limited. The prospect of going to the US offers Eilis new vistas – even if she is slightly sceptical about some of the associated myths about America as the land of unlimited opportunities. She is anxious about leaving home, having grown up to presume that she would always live in her home town, fearing the thought that she is going to lose this world for ever, excited but apprehensive for the future.

Eilis's experiences of migration turn out to be relatively positive. She finds her feet. And so she makes a new life for herself, improving her job prospects through going to night school to learn book keeping. And she comes to fall in love with a young Italian American whose family turns out to be warm and welcoming, whatever her initial fears about their cultural differences and potential prejudices (having been firmly told by her boyfriend's younger brother that 'We don't like Irish people' on her first visit to their family home).

Eilis does suffer from homesickness at first. After the initial excitement, she feels emotionally thrown by letters from home. 'It was as though an ache in her chest was trying to force tears down her cheeks despite her enormous effort to keep them back.... She was nobody here ... nothing here was part of her' (Toibin, 2009, pp 66-7). 'It was like hell, she thought, because she could see no end to it...' (Toibin, 2009, p 70). But as Father Flood explains, homesickness does pass. This is a success story so far.

Without giving too much of the plot away, Eilis's story becomes more complicated. On returning to Ireland for a family visit she discovers that circumstances have changed, with more opportunities becoming available. She also feels the pull of family and friends, together with the possibility of romance. So this time around, she has more effective choices. What to do? 'Eilis tried to pray and found herself actually answering the question that she was about to ask in her prayers. The answer was that there was no answer, that nothing she could do would be right' (Toibin, 2009, p. 236). The dilemma lies in the fact that she has realistic options back in Ireland as well as for a new life and for love in the US.

So Eilis's story illustrates some of the complexities involved in the processes of migration. There are economic push factors to be taken into account, due to the lack of job opportunities in Ireland at the time of her departure. And there are economic pull factors, with the wider opportunities to be taken up in the US. There are social factors involved, including the networks of support within the Irish community, networks that facilitate the migration process. And there are emotional factors involved, the ties of family and friends, not to forget the promise of love in both places. Eilis has some scope for making choices right from the start, despite the wider structural constraints. And these choices widen as the story develops.

Chapter Two's discussion of different approaches to the study of diaspora has already identified similar processes. How far had communities moved as a matter of choice, in pursuit of better livelihoods, in the past – economic migrants, in contemporary terms? How far had their moves been constrained by wider pressures, including the lack of opportunities for sustainable livelihoods, back home? And how had their situations and their feelings changed over time?

As Chapter Two went on to consider, there were parallel questions to be explored in relation to more recent and contemporary forms of displacement, including forcible displacement. Trafficked women and girls have been described as victims of modern slavery, as have trafficked men and boys, trapped in very precarious and often violent situations, experiencing forced labour practices as defined in UK and international law (Lewis et al, 2015). But there have also been counter arguments to be addressed. As O'Connell Davidson (2015) and others have pointed out, people do have agency, even in such challenging circumstances, making it difficult to fit them neatly into binary categories – trafficking/smuggling, slavery/freedom, victim/agent, or indeed, exploiter/exploited.

Public policies and choices too?

Whether people can be fitted into binary categories – or not – this is so often how they are categorised in practice, as the result of public policy decisions whether locally, nationally, or indeed, transnationally. As previous chapters have already pointed out, the UNHCR's distinction between economic migrants on the one hand, and refugees on the other, has an impact on national policies, just as this distinction has an impact on the ways in which newcomers are popularly perceived and treated within communities. The point to emphasise here is this. Public policies have been making a difference, sorting newcomers into different categories, distinguishing the (worthy?) sheep from the (less deserving?) goats, never mind identifying the potential terrorists, popularly supposed to be lurking among the latest arrivals from war-torn zones. These categorisations have an impact on people's lives, opening opportunities for some while closing off options for others.

The ways in which refugees have been confined in recent times provide particularly disturbing illustrations of the impacts of public policies on the lives of the most vulnerable. Refugees fleeing the civil war in Syria have been herded into camps and restrained behind barbed wire as they have attempted to move across European borders in search of safety. And refugee children have been kept 'in their place' in the 'Jungle' outside Calais – although this is not, of course, 'their place', having been *displaced* and in search of a place of safety with relatives in Britain. Their choices have been constrained by governments, whether these are governments perpetrating violence on their own citizens, intervening across national borders and/or intervening to seal their own borders against newcomers, regardless of their human needs.

So what about the scope for policy-makers to make choices themselves, more generally? What scope do they have for promoting agendas for social justice and solidarity, addressing the structural causes of dispersals, as well as addressing the more immediate effects?

As previous chapters have already suggested, neoliberal policies have been presented as the only game in town. But this is precisely the logic that Farnsworth and Irving (2015), among others, have been challenging. Without in any way minimising the threats that are being posed, there *are* other options to be pursued. The following chapter explores some of these alternative possibilities in further detail, working towards the development of more publicly accountable and potentially more transformative approaches to the promotion of social solidarity.

Before moving on to consider these, however, this chapter concludes by exploring ways in which people might be supported to maximise their agency as active citizens. What knowledge and skills might they need in order to address the causes of dispersal and dispossession most effectively, identifying the spaces for developing alternatives? And how might they be supported in sharing their knowledge and skills more widely, building alliances for more progressive approaches to public policies and practices? This brings the discussion to the potential contributions of community-based education, community development and community arts.

Popular education for social transformation

As the previous chapter has already suggested, people can and do learn from their experiences. And their learning can be supported and enhanced, enabling them to be more effective as active citizens. The goals of popular education have been precisely this, as defined by the Popular Education Forum for Scotland, being 'rooted in the real interests and struggles of ordinary people … overtly political and critical of the *status quo* … [and] committed to progressive social and political change' (Martin, 1999, p 4), focused on collective learning and attempting where possible to 'forge a direct link between education and social action' (Martin, 1999, p 5). This was precisely the type of approach to popular education that has been developed in Latin America (Kane, 2001) and elsewhere, drawing on the ideas of Gramsci, Freire and others (Freire, 1972; Gramsci, 1986; Ledwith, 2005), including popular educationalists who have applied these ideas through community arts practices (Boal, 1979, 1995; Clover and Sandford, 2013; Rooke, 2013; Tiller, 2013).

Starting from people's own priorities, the aim of popular education has been to unpack the root causes of popular concerns, challenging the accepted explanations of everyday 'common sense'. As Gramsci, Freire and others have demonstrated, power is not only about the ability to enforce your will on others (although it is about that too). Power can be exercised less directly, through social policies that set out to manage people's behaviours, for example, including those that attempt to control behaviours in line with neoliberal economic agendas, stigmatising 'dependency' and applying sanctions, with correspondingly damaging effects on the lives of low-income and vulnerable people as a result (Sanders, 2016). Power is also about knowledge and discourse (Foucault, 1991). And this includes the power to set agendas, defining which issues are – and most importantly which issues are *not* – up for negotiation or even for discussion (Lukes, 2004). Finally, power is also about the ways in which people discipline themselves (Foucault, 1991), internalising particular attitudes and norms. These include the patriarchal attitudes that are still being instilled into so many women and girls, for example, as well as in the minds of so many men – the 'cops in the head' that also need to be challenged (Boal, 1995).

John Gaventa's power cube has particular relevance here as a tool for popular education, enabling communities to explore the power structures that they need to address, at different levels, both externally and internally (Gaventa, 2006). This power cube brings these different aspects of power together, setting them out in the form of a Rubik's cube, representing the different levels, spaces and forms of power:

The levels of power at:

- the global
- the national and
- the local.

The spaces of power that are:

- closed (where decisions are taken behind closed doors, away from public scrutiny)
- invited (such as public consultation spaces where people may be invited to participate) and
- claimed or created (where communities have gained access, opening previously closed spaces up for public engagement).

The different forms of power:

- visible (as with government structures, for example)

- hidden (as with the issues that never emerge on public agendas, because they are being resolved behind closed doors) or
- invisible (the attitudes that are internalised, and the self-limitations that ensue – Boal's 'cop in the head').

If we want to change power relationships, to make them more inclusive or pro-poor, Gaventa maintains, 'we must understand more about where and how to engage' in differing contexts (Gaventa, 2006, p 23), enabling citizens to recover a sense of their capacity to act. The power cube provides a tool for 'actors seeking to change the world to reflect on where and how they do so, and how they work across boundaries with others who are also working for change' (Gaventa, 2006, p 31), finding the spaces for change within wider structural constraints.

Community-based campaigns to resist displacement have involved precisely such processes. The importance of understanding – and knowing how to engage with – different levels of power emerges in the Indian stories of challenges to the construction of big dams, for example, involving international as well as national and more local organisations and agencies (Roy, 1999). The role of trusted NGOs was significant in similar contexts, supporting local people to develop 'Alternative Development Plans', representing their interests to maximum effect at public hearings (Newell and Wheeler, 2006).

The importance of understanding the different spaces of power has particular relevance, too, as the stories of community-based resistance to redevelopment in London illustrated. The amount of genuinely affordable housing that was to be provided was being negotiated behind closed doors, invisible to public scrutiny. But community activists effectively challenged these closed decision-making processes, arguing that developers should not be allowed to hide behind veils of secrecy, claiming that their schemes lacked commercial viability without providing evidence for their assertions. Building on local knowledge, experience and skills, backed up with professional expertise, community activists had succeeded in bringing these issues out into the open, going on to share their expertise with others facing similar challenges elsewhere.

And the varying forms taken by power have had relevance too. The visible structures of power have emerged across so many of the stories, but so have some of the less visible aspects. Women and girls' fears of violence affected their attitudes and behaviours, effectively keeping them firmly within their places in the Indian context, for example. Tackling these aspects of power has involved engaging with people's attitudes and emotions, enabling them to explore alternatives in safety – before going on to challenge such attitudes and fears more publicly.

This is one of the contexts in which community arts have particularly relevant contributions to add. As Darlene Clover, Kathy Sandford and their colleagues have demonstrated, the arts and cultural engagement can and do contribute to community development (Clover and Sandford, 2013), facilitating learning for social change across a range of contexts internationally. Through providing a mode of expression and a space for critical pedagogy, community arts 'can encourage and develop active citizenship and empowerment', with arts organisations and artists acting as 'important players in the revitalisation of communities' (Rooke, 2013, p 151) and the promotion of social cohesion. The arts can stimulate people to question previously accepted ways of seeing their worlds, provoking critical thinking (Tiller, 2013). And engagement with community arts can lead to 'raised levels of self-esteem and confidence, an enhanced feeling of self-determination and control' (Rooke, 2013, p 165).

Community arts can involve people in critical, participatory ways – although they are not necessarily provided in participative or critical ways, of course. On the contrary. But where they are, they can strengthen people's abilities to exercise their agency to maximum effect, both individually and collectively, with particular relevance for women when it comes to addressing the more invisible aspects of power (English and Irving, 2015).

Augusto Boal's development of participatory theatre provides a case in point, offering a set of tools that can be adapted for differing contexts, to promote individual therapies as well as more collective forms of social change (Boal, 1979, 1995). Boal set out to challenge the barriers between actors and spectators: 'all must act', he argued, 'all must be protagonists in the necessary transformations of society' (Boal, 1979, Foreword).

The process starts by developing a street theatre play based on an issue that local people have themselves identified as a priority. Once the play has been performed, the audience is then invited to participate more directly. The performance is then replayed. But this time members of the audience can interrupt the actors, coming on to the stage to act out alternative scenarios, exploring other ways of addressing the issue in question in order to achieve a more satisfactory outcome. A number of different approaches may then be tried before the audience comes to any kind of conclusion as to the most appropriate way forward.

Boal provided examples from participatory drama to illustrate some of the numerous ways in which the community arts can support people to act, both individually and collectively, as agents for social change. As Boal himself demonstrated, the arts can engage with the world of emotions, a capacity with particular relevance when it comes to addressing the less visible aspects of power. Whether the process is as effective when it comes to the more visible structures of power and decision-making may be more debatable, however. I had the opportunity to participate in a session in which Boal demonstrated the application of his method through what he termed 'legislative theatre' (Boal, 1998). Here the process involved the audience in testing out different policy solutions to the problems that were being presented.

In the London context (which is where this particular event took place), I wondered whether the method would be sufficiently sensitive to the complexities of the relevant policy processes. Would it be able to address the levels and structures of power involved in an issue such as homelessness, for example, one of the topics that we explored? Members of the audience tried out different roles in a scenario involving a young homeless person in search of bed for the night, meeting with unhelpful responses from an overworked hostel warden. The method worked well at this level, enabling the audience to explore ways of engaging with front-line professionals more effectively.

But would the method work so well as a tool for exploring the development of alternative strategies at national and regional levels, in order to tackle the root causes of homelessness in contemporary urban contexts? I was less sure. But Boal applied the method directly himself as a tool for developing policies to tackle people's priority problems when he became a local government councillor in Sao Paulo, Brazil. And he maintained that the method worked very well in this context, leading to a number of practical legislative changes. Differing methods and approaches may need to be tailored to be fit-for-purpose, depending on the issues to be addressed, at which levels and spaces and in what forms.

To conclude more generally, as Amartya Sen has reflected:

> ... even when the freedoms that a woman (or for that matter, a man) can exercise to make deliberate decisions are constrained and even when the power to carry out those decisions is also restricted, these freedoms and powers are not typically entirely absent. (quoted in Dasgupta and Lal, 2007, pp 355-6)

Women had rebelled courageously, he pointed out, emphasising that we can fail to exercise our freedoms by taking our decisional powers to be even more limited than they actually are. 'Fear is sometimes more crippling that reality' (quoted in Dasgupta and Lal, 2007, p 356).

What people in adverse positions can achieve, he continued, also depends on whether they act alone or with others. 'There is strength in the unity of the deprived and underprivileged' (quoted in Dasgupta and Lal, 2007, p 7). Amartya Sen was referring to popular protests against big dam projects in the Indian context, but his conclusions about the importance of understanding the scope for human agency, both as individuals and as members of communities, would seem to have relevance more widely.

SEVEN

The slippery concept of 'community', both locally and transnationally

The concept of 'community' has long been contested, as Stacey pointed out, way back in 1969. Having identified 94 different usages, it was doubtful, in her view, as to 'whether the concept "community" refers to a useful abstraction at all' (Stacey, 1969, p 134). But this inherent ambiguity does not seem to have inhibited its use. On the contrary, such slipperiness may have constituted part of its charm for those concerned with developing public policies, sprayed with community's associated warm glow. 'Community' policies sound more caring perhaps, even if these are policies to decrease the provision of public resources or to increase the level of surveillance at the local level. This chapter starts out by re-summarising the main usages of the term, together with the main points of contention, taking account of the darker, exclusionary sides along with the warmer, cosier usages.

Having re-summarised the main ways in which the term has been applied so far, the chapter moves on to explore some of the potential implications in relation to processes of migration, displacement and dispossession. Communities form and re-form themselves, in differing circumstances and at different levels, locally and beyond, transnationally, processes of change that suggest the need for expanding previous definitions accordingly. Public policies have an impact on these processes in varying ways – for better or indeed for worse – as the chapter goes on to suggest. And so do market forces, as the penultimate example also illustrates.

Differing definitions and varying usages

So far in the discussion the concept of 'community' has generally been applied in three main ways:

- community as locality (typically referring to neighbourhoods in urban areas, or villages in more rural contexts)
- community as identity (such as identities of race and ethnicity) and
- community as shared interests (such as mutual support groups).

These are familiar distinctions, as found in key community work texts, but such definitions have also been described as 'elusive, imprecise, contradictory and controversial' (Popple, 2015, p 18), slippery, and shifting, in varying contexts over time and space. So what more, if anything, might need to be said? Haven't these distinctions already been done over to death? I used to think so.

The more that I think about these debates, however, the more questions that emerge concerning their continuing relevance in the contemporary context. Might these earlier definitions need to be revisited, in order to take account of the impacts of globalisation – and the varying ways in which communities have been coming together, in response to their experiences of migration, dispersal and dispossession, coming apart and then reconstituting themselves, both locally and transnationally – which suggests the need for further unpacking, to take account of such shifts in meanings and usages over time and space?

Starting from Raymond Williams' approach

Raymond Williams' collection of commentaries on *Keywords* (Williams, 1988) included an entry on the history of the varying usages of the term 'community'. This has provided a useful starting point from which to explore the debates and emotional connotations that have surrounded – and continue to surround – the term. Williams pointed out that the term 'community' had been in the English language since the 14th century, originally referring to the 'common people' rather than referring to those of rank or to the state. While usages have shifted considerably since then, elements of such populist associations linger – 'the community' as ordinary people, as in the context of 'community' responses to official edicts from on high, the 'grass roots' rather than 'the suits and frocks', to use more contemporary terms.

From the 19th century, the term was also being used to distinguish local, face-to-face 'communities' from the larger, more complex relationships that were emerging in urban industrial societies. There are traces of nostalgia here, harking back to romanticised images of rural idylls, 'imagined' communities of a bygone era, emotive implications with continuing resonance in the contemporary context, as with debates about decentralisation, for example.

This focus on the local continues into more recent times. The term is so often still applied to refer to neighbourhoods, whether or not their inhabitants share common identities and interests in practice. On the contrary, in fact. They may be divided by differences of class, caste, gender and sexuality, just as they may include differing interests, depending on people's age, ethnicity, ability and faith. And there may be significant power differentials within as well as between these varying and intersecting interests, recognising that 'concrete social locations are constructed along multiple (and both shifting and contingent) axes of difference' (Dhaliwal and Yuval-Davis, 2014, p 35). In other words, people's positions depend on interlocking differences, as Dhaliwal and Yuval-Davis have gone on to explain. 'Class cannot be experienced or lived outside of "race", gender, sexuality and the same is true of other categories', in their view (p 35).

As Chapter Two has already illustrated, power differentials can also shift over time and place, as people move within and across national borders. Men may fear the loss of power when taking refuge in new contexts – for example, Somali men describing Denmark as 'a ladies' country' (Kleist, 2010), whatever the realities in question. While the relatively powerful, in contrast, may be able to strengthen their positions still further, through migration (Holton, 2008), potentially exacerbating divisions and conflicts in the process. So communities of identity are typically heterogeneous too. Like communities of locality, communities of identity are typically characterised by power imbalances, differentials that may shift over time in response to people's experiences of migration, displacement and dispossession.

Finally, Williams concluded that 'community' tends to be used in what he described as warmly persuasive ways, whether referring to existing relationships in the present or alternative relationships for the future, with greater emphasis on mutuality, along with increasing emphasis on participation and collective engagement (Williams, 1988, p 76). The reality has been somewhat different, however. 'Community' has *also* been associated more negatively with social problems in urban policy contexts, 'problem communities' in need of treatment (Matthews and O'Brien, 2016), as previous chapters have already illustrated.

Elena Ferrante's Neapolitan novel cycle (Ferrante, 2012) provides particularly striking illustrations of community's darker sides, along with the ambivalent feelings of *Those who leave and those who stay* (the title of the third novel in the cycle) – community as security from the hostile world outside versus community as a trap, keeping people in their disadvantaged places. The novels tell the stories of Elena and Lila, two friends growing up in a poor neighbourhood, a tightly knit community around Naples. As Elena, the narrator, explains, from the outset, 'I feel no nostalgia for our childhood: it was full of violence' (Ferrante, 2012, p 37). But this was how it was, she adds. 'I don't recall having ever thought that the life we had there was particularly bad' (Ferrante, 2012, p 37). 'Life was like that, that's all, we grew up with the duty to make it difficult for others before they made it difficult for us' (Ferrante, 2012, p 37), the imperative to hit first rather than waiting to be hit by others. This was a basic lesson, but one that the radical middle-class students who subsequently came south, to engage in community organising, failed to understand, to their cost, getting beaten up as a result, as a subsequent novel in the cycle goes on to recount.

Elena herself would have liked the nice manners that the teacher and the priest preached, she explains, but 'I felt that those ways were not suited to our neighbourhood, even if you were a girl. The women fought among themselves more than the men, they pulled each other's hair, they hurt each other' (Ferrante, 2012, p 37). While the men were always getting furious, Elena continues, 'they calmed down in the end; women, who appeared to be silent, acquiescent, when they were angry flew into a rage that had no end' (Ferrante, 2012, p 38).

As the novel cycle develops, the two friends make different choices, to leave the community for a different life with wider opportunities elsewhere, or to stay, surviving, if not eventually thriving, through marrying into a relatively wealthy family with illicit 'camorra' connections (the 'camorra' being the Neapolitan version of the Mafia).

Nadine Gordimer's most recent novel, *No time like the present* (Gordimer, 2012), provides further aspects of community's darker sides, along with the varying perceptions of people's responses to migration, depending on their colour and social class. The novel's protagonists, Steven and Jabulile, are a mixed race couple, both of whom have been engaged in struggles against apartheid. Now living in a comfortable suburb, surrounded by a community of former comrades and friends, they seem to be doing so well, despite the wider frustrations of rising racial and political tensions in post-apartheid South Africa.

There is increasing violence, however, including violence directed at migrants and refugees from neighbouring Zimbabwe. So what are the Comrades in the suburb going to do about it, 'we companeros of the Suburb ... round the any-colour, any-race, any-sex swimming pool' (Gordimer, 2012, p 204), they wonder – this suburban community faced with surrounding communities of hatred. 'Xenophobia, African hating African?' (Gordimer, 2012, p 204). The view that 'they are only here to steal … they tell lies why they come here…. Everybody must stay at their country to make it right, not run away', as her relatives argue, to Jabulile's dismay (Gordimer, 2012, pp 204-5).

In the event, the couple come to shelter a wounded refugee, a Zimbabwean twice displaced, 'first the long rough trial escape from conflict and hunger bringing your country to ruin, then rejection in a brother country' (Gordimer, 2012, p 410). The couple share 'the same intense conception of horror at the degradation to violence people have descended against Zimbabweans' (Gordimer, 2012, p 411), Steven adding reflections on what might have happened to him, too, if he had been born a generation earlier and in Europe, with his thread of Jewish blood. But in his present context he has different choices. Unlike the Zimbabweans, he can flee the violence and be welcomed as an immigrant elsewhere. 'Migrants sought to stimulate economy', the publicity reads, encouraging 'desirables', 'people with degrees' like him to leave for Australia (Gordimer, 2012, p 247).

Perceptions of migrant communities vary so much depending on which type of community is being perceived by whom. There have been communities of expatriates in southern Spain who have been able to choose to live in British enclaves without attempting to integrate with their Spanish neighbours, for example, let alone attempting to learn their language, behaviours that would be widely criticised as unacceptable for migrants coming *to* Britain from elsewhere. Caroline Knowles and Douglas Harper's study of migrant lives, landscapes and journeys provides similar stories of British expatriate communities, this time in post-colonial Hong Kong (Knowles and Harper, 2009). These are 'lifestyle migrants', so-called because they have aspirations for a desirable lifestyle as expatriates, whatever the differences between them in terms of their origins and previous experiences. Some are described as 'recycled colonial functionaries who arrived in the seventies to work the apparatus of empire and its attendant enterprises as police officers, civil engineers or teachers' (Knowles and Harper, 2009, p 13). They have decided to stay on. Others are described as more recent arrivals with a range of occupational backgrounds. But despite their differences, as the authors explain, 'those outside of the main corporate matrix of global business operate in a small niche' of an expatriate community (Knowles and Harper, 2009, p 13).

As one of the younger generation of those who were interviewed recounted, '(W)e're in our own little bubble here, you know: an international community of us Westerners' (quoted in Knowles and Harper, 2009, p 51). The Chinese 'they don't think much of us' she continues, 'I mean, there's no interaction really' (quoted in Knowles and Harper, 2009, p 51). But this isn't seen as too much of an issue. Life inside the expatriate lifestyle bubble is comfortable, even if somewhat lonely.

This is very different, in contrast, from the varied lives of those who migrate from the Philippines and elsewhere as domestic service workers. Their communities are perceived very differently, reflecting their ethnicity and class positions in Hong Kong. Their relationships with Chinese communities are described as 'intimate, restricted, and subordinate' (Knowles and Harper, 2009, p 171).

Diasporic communities have similarly varied experiences, depending on their social situations as well as their geographical origins. And they have been having similarly varied effects on their communities of origin, as previous chapters have already suggested. Diasporas can contribute to community development initiatives back home, of course, but they can also exacerbate conflicts, as Martha Nussbaum reflected, analysing the causes of the mass murders of Muslims in Gujarat, India, in 2002 (Nussbaum, 2007). 'The US (Indian) diaspora is and will remain an important part of Indian politics', she argued (Nussbaum, 2007, p 328). 'This community has the potential for great good, particularly in the areas of poverty and disaster relief…. [But i]t also has the potential for great harm', she continued, pointing to the diaspora community's scope for exacerbating communalisation and communal conflict (Nussbaum, 2007, p 328).

Even so, despite such powerful evidence of community's darker sides, whether locally or transnationally, much of the discourse has indeed been more positively focused. So why has this been the case? Bauman examined this question further (2001), exploring the reasons for such romanticism, which he particularly associated with the context in which he was writing, at the beginning of the 21st century, with population movements on massive scales, movements of labour as well as forcible displacements in the context of neoliberal globalisation.

Communities have been perceived as warm places, in Bauman's view, despite rather than because of the actual complexities of people's experiences in practice. This was because the idea of 'community' represents the 'kind of world which is not, regrettably available to us' (Bauman, 2001, p 3), a search for security and safety in an insecure and rapidly changing world. There are parallels here with Richard Sennett's view of the notion of communities as promising islands of homely and cosy tranquillity in a sea of turbulence and inhospitality, suggesting nostalgic alternatives to the alienation of contemporary capitalism (Sennett, 1976).

Bauman himself concluded his study by focusing on the continuing need for 'community' in a world of individuals, suggesting that an acceptable balance might be achieved with a community 'woven together from sharing and mutual care', a community that was also based on 'concern for the equal right to be human and the equal ability to act on that right' (Bauman, 2001, p 150).

Community and public policy

But the notion of 'community' can, of course, be applied in other ways, too, with less emphasis on human rights and more on promoting consensus – contemporary versions of 'motherhood and apple pie'. This has certainly been the view of a number of critics, sceptical of the ways in which 'community' has been sprayed on, to sugar the pill of potentially unpalatable public policy developments. Community care has been an obvious target for such criticisms, for instance, along with community policing, masking agendas to reduce public service provision while maintaining and enhancing social control.

Community development programmes have been similarly contentious (Craig, 2008, 2016), adding a 'confusing gloss' to policy processes that were 'as much concerned with controlling and determining the direction of change in communities facing crisis as with enabling people to take greater control of their lives' (Jackson, 1995, p 183). As Shaw and Martin subsequently reflected on this view, such analyses drew attention 'to both the ambivalent nature of state policy and the ambivalent positioning of the community worker within it' (Shaw and Martin, 2008, pp 298-9), emphasising the inherent contradictions involved, both for better and indeed for worse. These ambivalences have increasing relevance in the context of neoliberal austerity policies, as communities are being encouraged to engage in self-help initiatives, volunteering to span the widening gaps between increasing social needs on the one hand, and decreasing public service provision on the other (Milbourne, 2013; Kenny et al, 2015).

This is in no way to undervalue the contributions that community development programmes have made, however; on the contrary. Community development programmes have supported communities in a variety of ways over time, enabling people to come together more effectively to address their common concerns. Community development interventions have set out to bring people together, to build a sense of community, and to address problems of poverty and social deprivation in the wake of industrial restructuring, as in the case of the Community Development Programme (CDP) in Britain, widening the programme's initial remit in challenging ways in the process (Craig, 2008, 2016). People have agency, as the previous chapter has already argued – and this includes community development workers and community education and arts workers as well as those they work alongside.

Marilyn Taylor and Mandy Wilson's reflections on the British coalition government's initiatives to promote community organising through training 500 community organisers provide more recent illustrations (Taylor and Wilson, 2016). This programme has had its detractors. Much was being achieved within localities in their view, however, despite the programme's official constraints. Most organisers focused their efforts on building community: 'They brought people together, built relationships, restored a sense of community and focused on existing resources' (Fisher and Dimberg, 2016, p 102). But this was far from being the total picture: 'Other organizers utilized direct action, to help communities meet their needs' (Fisher and Dimberg, 2016, p 102). Campaigns were beginning to emerge, drawing on experiences of organising within the programme: 'It turned out that the modest goals and limited supervision (not to mention the absence of expected bureaucratic burdens) allowed for organizer autonomy and latitude to pursue different approaches and issues' (Fisher and Dimberg, 2016, p 102).

Marilyn Taylor and Mandy Wilson similarly referred to the emergence of different approaches, including campaigns on access to decent, secure and affordable housing. They reflected that 'one successor initiative has 1,600 people signed up in the part of the city where it is based and is about to go citywide, while another is building national awareness and harnessing widespread support through both social and mainstream media' (Taylor and Wilson, 2016, p 227). As a journalist commented, reflecting on their achievements, this was 'The year the grassroots took on the powerful – and won. Ignored communities have forced the elites to listen' by getting organised (Taylor and Wilson, 2016, p 227).

There have been both positive and negative sides to public policies in the community, just as there have been dark sides as well as warmly emotive sides to the concept of community itself. As Sue Kenny and others have pointed out, communities 'can be based around strong feelings of mutuality and solidarity' (Kenny et al, 2015, p 40). But they can be exclusive and discriminatory, as previous chapters have illustrated. They can be fearful and aggressive towards others, generating intercommunal conflict and violence. And they can be controlling, providing spaces for the exercise of power, legitimising the claims of *some* to represent the interests of *others*.

So 'community' continues to be debated as a contested concept. Previous debates have continuing relevance, highlighting some of the emotional connotations. But previous debates also need to be expanded to have continuing relevance in contemporary contexts. The notion of 'community' needs to be explored at different levels, taking account of communities that cross borders internationally, as well as those that remain located at the neighbourhood level. People have multiple attachments, and the 'local' isn't the only focus for many, as Marilyn Taylor and Mandy Wilson concluded (Taylor and Wilson, 2016). People can and do identify with differing communities, in varying ways, over space and time.

Community formation – and re-formation – in response to displacement and dispossession

So how have communities been developing in practice, whether these have been communities of place, of identity or of common interests or some combination of each, forming and re-forming in response to people's experiences of displacement and dispossession? As Chapter Two has already pointed out, people's identifications with their communities of place have been centrally important factors in their decisions about migration. People have been moving to places with prospects of community support, just as they have been moving in search of livelihoods, enabling them to send remittances back to their communities of origin. Migration processes have strengthened community ties and the development of diasporas in some contexts, with powerful pressures to respond to the 'early morning call', as studies of Somali communities have demonstrated, for example (Lindley, 2010). But migration processes have loosened community identifications and ties in other contexts too.

As the writer, Stefan Zweig, reflected, Jewish diaspora communities may have held together in the past, bound together by their religion and culture – communities of identity. But this was no longer the case, in his experience. '(T)he Jews of the twentieth century were not a community any more, nor had they been for a long time' (Zweig, 2011, pp 453-4) in his view. Jews (cosmopolitan intellectual Jews like himself?) were 'increasingly impatient to integrate with the lives of the peoples around them and become part of their communities', he continued, 'dispersing into society in general, if only to have some relief from persecution and rest instead of moving on – they were more French, German, British and Russian than they were Jews' (Zweig, 2011, p 454). Zweig himself had felt similarly dissociated from being Jewish, as he explained in his autobiography, although from an internationalist rather than a nationalist perspective. But all this was to change in the 1930s, with the growth of virulent anti-Semitism. 'Only now', Zweig reflected, 'were Jews forced, for the first time in centuries, to be a single community again. It was a long time since they had felt like that', he added, 'a community of outcasts driven out again and again since the exile from Egypt' (Zweig, 2011, p 454).

In her recent autobiography, Lillian Rosengarten similarly explained the complexity of her own identity as a German Jewish refugee from Nazi Germany. As she grew up in the US she described herself as having 'haphazardly identified as a "cultural Jew"', holding on to a mere 'vestige of her Jewish identification' (Rosengarten, 2015, p 22). Years later, she explained, she visited relatives in Israel, which she came to see as a 'beacon of light ... a safe haven and land of compassion where refugees everywhere would be welcome' (Rosengarten, 2015, p 22). This matched her own longing for a safe homeland, with socialist-style communal living, a community of warmth and solidarity in an insecure world. 'I wanted to love Israel, where I had felt safe, free and happy to be Jewish', she continued (Rosengarten 2015, p 23), echoing some of Bauman's reflections on community and the search for safety in an insecure and rapidly changing world. But her dream became tainted as her identification as a refugee 'became a driving force in my empathy with the victimization and struggle of Palestinians; 700,000 Palestinians were thrown out in 1948, and those who have not died remain as homeless refugees' (Rosengarten, 2015, p 23). This had been a soul-searching journey, she explained, leading her to become an active campaigner for Palestinian rights.

So people's identifications with their communities of identity can be multifaceted. And they can and do shift over space and time. Experiences of displacement and dispossession as a result of violence can bring people together just as such experiences can drive communities apart. Dispersals and dispossessions can result from intercommunal violence, of course, but communities can also develop strategies to build bridges across such divides, whatever the challenges involved, as previous chapters have also suggested (Cockburn, 1998, 2012). And communities have been forming and re-forming themselves, in response to the threat of dispersal from development pressures too, whether in urban, semi-urban or rural contexts.

Migration, dispersal and dispossession, including the threat of dispersal and dispossession, have varying impacts. People's identifications with particular communities vary, whether these are communities based on localities, villages or neighbourhoods or on shared identities and interests. People have fluid, multiple identities rather than an 'essential' identity, as Stuart Hall and others have already argued (Hall, 1991), just as the cultures with which they identify develop with fluidity over time (Gilroy, 1987, 1993). As Hall has also pointed out, 'identities are never completed, never finished; they are always as subjectivity itself is, in process' (Hall, 1991, p 47) – and similarly with collectivities more generally. 'We always reconstructed them more essentially, more homogenously, more unified, less contradictorily than they ever were', in Hall's view (Hall, 1991, p 46). People's identifications shift, as communities form and re-form themselves in differing locations. And interests within communities vary, with the potential for increasing conflict, within as well as between them, as well as the potential for building increasing collaboration and solidarity across differences.

How have these outcomes been affected by public policies?

Previous chapters have already illustrated a range of ways in which public policies have had an impact on communities. Locally based communities have been displaced as the direct result of public policies to promote development and urban redevelopment, for example, whether displacement has been the intention or not. Such forms of displacement have long histories, including the history of the redevelopment processes that transformed the old East End of London, for example, following the bombings of the Second World War (Young and Willmott, 1957).

Young and Willmott's research highlighted the ways in which close family and kinship ties, in what they described as a village community in the middle of London, could be fractured as a result of redevelopment initiatives, leaving those who moved to new council estates on the outskirts of the city feeling 'cut off from their relatives, suspicious of neighbours, lonely' (Young and Willmott, 1957, p 7). Subsequent research demonstrated that people in the suburbs could and indeed did form their own communities, however, rebuilding ties of neighbourliness in new localities. 'People in the suburbs are on the whole friendly, neighbourly and helpful to each other', they concluded (Willmott and Young, 1971, p 7).

Willmott and Young also recognised the ways in which class divisions affected the development of local communities, as working-class newcomers tended to be stigmatised. 'We don't tell people we come from Bethnal Green', explained one woman, for example, 'You get the scum of the earth there', it was said (quoted in Willmott and Young, 1971, p 15).

When researchers revisited the old East End in the first decade of the 21st century, they also identified further tensions. This time it was white working-class people who were expressing resentment against newcomers. Bangladeshi people were being blamed for their own poverty and social exclusion, fuelled by the belief that newcomers were getting priority in terms of access to public services. Middle-class public service providers were described as 'those big-hearted ones who've got their own big houses and make these rules' (about the allocation of services such as council housing) (Dench et al, 2006, p 6).

Public policy interventions have particular relevance for communities in the current context, whether the focus is urban redevelopment and renewal, or on the allocation of services and the impact in terms of community cohesion more generally. There can be particularly detrimental effects in terms of exacerbating competition and conflicts *within* as well as *between* communities. And these tensions can be re-enforced as the result of public policies towards newcomers, as exclusionary interventions to control immigration demonstrate, thereby enabling unscrupulous employers to undermine local pay and conditions by employing undocumented labour. Far from being coincidental, Lewis and colleagues have argued,

> … labour exploitation is intimately connected to an increasingly draconian immigration policy regime that purposefully restricts the rights of newly arrived migrants, whether from the newest member states of an enlarged European Union (EU), or the growing humanitarian disaster zones of the Global South. (Lewis et al, 2015, p 3)

These humanitarian disaster zones are not without their public policy connections either, foreign policy interventions having been major factors, causing mass population movements of people fleeing from the ensuing conflicts in search of safety and security for themselves and their families.

As Hickman and others have also pointed out, 'there is no more febrile issue in British politics than immigration, apart maybe from terrorism (and the two are often interlinked)' (Hickman et al, 2012, p 1). And that was written back in 2012, before more recent terrorist atrocities, just as this was before the refugee crisis sparked off by the civil war in Syria. Newcomers are all too readily scapegoated, along with other 'marginal' groups, stereotyped as welfare scroungers if not actually branded as violent extremists, with migrant youth particularly at risk from experiencing humiliation and social exclusion (Tyler, 2013). There are parallels here with the stigmatisation of the poor more generally (Tyler, 2013), stereotyping the most vulnerable sections of the white working class as 'chavs' (Jones, 2011). In Tyler's view, the urban conflicts of 2011 were not just about poverty or police repression, although those were indeed explanatory factors; these conflicts were also revolts against stigmatisation (Tyler, 2013).

Politicians can all too easily exacerbate the resulting tensions within and between communities, as previous chapters have also illustrated, starting with the case of civil war in Nigeria in the 1960s, as outlined in Chapter One. The disturbing rise in reported hate crimes in Britain in 2016 provides a more recent example, illustrating the toxic effects of a xenophobic campaign to persuade the electorate to vote against Britain's continuing membership of the EU.

The following chapter explores policies to facilitate alternative outcomes, in contrast, focusing on policies to promote social cohesion and social solidarity – whether addressing the causes as well as the consequences of inequalities and injustices or not. But first, some reflections on the role of market forces and the ways in which these may be being re-enforced or might be, at least partially, contained via public policy interventions to support people in building new intentional communities of choice.

What about market forces?

So far discussion has focused on the varying ways in which public policies have been having an impact on communities, along with the varying impacts of market forces against the background of processes of dispersal and dispossession. But market forces and public policies have been having an impact in other ways too. Initiatives to *construct* intentional communities afresh have also encountered barriers from both, as experiences with developing co-housing projects illustrate, for example.

So what are intentional communities such as co-housing schemes about, and why do people choose to construct them? Raymond Williams' discussion of the concept of community's association with alternative ways of living and being has relevance here, emphasising the importance of participation and collective engagement with shared commitments to facilitating more caring and mutually supportive ways of living and being.

The construction of just such a 'community' has been a central aim for co-housing projects in North American and European contexts. As the UK Cohousing Network's website explains, 'Cohousing communities are created and run by their residents. Each household has a self-contained, private home but residents come together to manage their community and share activities' (http://cohousing.org. uk). In this way, the website continues, 'the alienation and isolation many experience today' may be combated, 'recreating the neighbourly support of the past.' A cohousing community typically involves between 8 and 40 households, some of them consisting of different age groups while others focus on particular groups, such as older people and 'communities of interest', such as older women or lesbian and gay people. Cohousing schemes include 'communities of interest' as well as being based 'first and foremost where people live' (http://cohousing. org.uk) in geographical neighbourhoods.

As Durrett's handbook for those with an interest in 'senior cohousing' reflects, in addition, 'Cohousing communities are unique in their extensive use of common facilities' (such as a common house where people share meals and other activities) 'and – most importantly – in that they are organized, planned and managed by the residents themselves' (Durrett, 2009, p 15).

Cohousing Woodside

This has been centrally important to the mission of Cohousing Woodside, a project in which I have been personally involved. As their website explains, 'Cohousing Woodside is a democratic and participatory group.' The vision is 'To create a community that is sustainable, inclusive and diverse, where people participate, have their own space, share resources and are proud and happy with where they live' (https://cohousingwoodside.co.uk). 'To us, building the community is as important as developing the building.' Intentional communities such as these cover many facets of 'community' – community as place, identity and interest, along with 'community' as alternative, participatory and mutually supportive ways of living and being. Far from being displaced or facing the threat of displacement, these cohousing groups come together as a matter of choice.

In the case of Cohousing Woodside, members have worked hard at building a shared sense of community. There have been workshops to develop common approaches to decision-making, for example, exploring ways of balancing individual needs and collective interests. There have been visits to other cohousing projects to learn from their experiences of building their communities, as well as learning from their experiences of organising their projects together, over a number of years. And there have been regular opportunities to develop a sense of community, more informally, over shared meals and social events. But the group has been facing a number of challenges.

The cohousing buildings have been for sale rather than for rent. This has limited access to those in a position to buy their home, significantly reducing the scope for ensuring a socially inclusive mix. Public resources could have been deployed to achieve such a mix by including genuinely affordable social housing for rent, but this had not been an option, understandably perhaps, given the financial context for the providers of social housing.

While this particular scheme worked in partnership with a housing association, housing associations have been under increasing pressure to become more marketised themselves, as previous chapters have already pointed out. When prices rose significantly over the course of the development process, a number of the members became unable to afford to continue.

The remaining Cohousing Woodside members responded by making determined efforts to recruit new members, committed to rebuilding the intentional community within the original time frame. But the situation was further complicated by market uncertainties in the run-up to the referendum on Britain's membership of the EU in June 2016. Another example of the effects of market forces both locally and beyond – an intentional community that has had to cope with a number of losses as a result of rising housing prices, followed by increasing uncertainties around the referendum. These effects have included the loss of a number of the founding members before any of them had even had the opportunity to move in.

LILAC: a cohousing project with 20 affordable homes in Bramley, Leeds

While market forces proved so problematic for this particular north London project, other projects have been more successful. Intentional communities *can* be developed through cohousing initiatives. And they *can* be developed in ways that focus on affordability as well as ecological sustainability (Chatterton, 2015), although this involves addressing a series of challenges in the process.

LILAC stands for 'low impact living affordable community'. When the book that tells LILAC's story was being written by one of the co-founders in 2013, some six years later, the cohousing scheme was finally up and running, providing 20 affordable homes and a common house in Bramley, Leeds. This has been described as 'one of a small breed of happy projects around the country that serve as exemplars of how we might build not just affordable homes but thriving, social and sustaining communities' (McCloud, quoted in Chatterton, 2015, Foreword).

Values were central to the project, the co-founders emphasised. This was to be based on principles of environmental sustainability, self-reliance, learning, equality, diversity and wellbeing, rooted in a shared understanding of the challenges involved in building communities. As the field guide explains, 'communities do not simply appear' (Chatterton, 2015, p 25). 'They are built patiently and slowly and through much deliberation and negotiation', addressing communities' inherent differences and divisions. As this account continues, 'to do otherwise [than to deliberate and negotiate around such differences] is to exclude, silence and marginalize' (Chatterton, 2015, p 25), quoting Bauman's view that the idea of a community would always generate tensions between group security on the one hand, and individual freedom on the other.

Community building was central to the development of LILAC. But so were the more directly material aspects, from planning and designing the project through to building the strawbale homes and the common house. One of the biggest challenges was to ensure that the housing would be genuinely affordable. How could the effects of a highly unequal and precarious financial system, with speculative and inflationary housing markets, be avoided?

Rather than working in partnership with a housing association, LILAC opted for an innovative form of tenure, Mutual Home Ownership. Without going into detail here, the point to emphasise is simply this, that LILAC's form of Mutual Home Ownership, financed with a loan from an ethical bank, has enabled the project to provide homes at the cost of no more than 35% of their residents' net incomes. This represented a major step forward in terms of social inclusivity. Even so, however, 'LILAC is affordable only within certain parameters', as the co-founders recognised (Chatterton, 2015, p 136). As they explained, 'it's a fine balancing act to ensure that all income profiles can service the total debt' (Chatterton, 2015, p 137). Over time, the hope was to make LILAC affordable to those on lower incomes too, but even with the present limitations, this was still far more successful as a financial model than the housing association partnership model had proved, in terms of addressing the challenge of affordability in Cohousing Woodside.

Summarising the factors that enabled LILAC to succeed more generally, the field guide pointed to the group's pioneering and inclusive vision. This had been accompanied by sustained determination with six years of incredibly hard work. Bringing in professionals with expertise at the right time had been vital. And so had the support that LILAC had received from statutory agencies, in their case, Leeds

City Council and the UK government's Homes and Communities Agencies. Together, they succeeded in holding market forces at bay, facilitating the development of an intentional community that was to be both affordable and environmentally sustainable.

As the book that tells LILAC's story explained at the outset, the aim was to provide a 'warts and all' account of the challenges involved. This had been a difficult and complex process (Chatterton, 2015, p 2). LILAC was absolutely not claiming to offer panaceas, as one of the other co-founders emphasised in parallel, when I had the opportunity to share reflections with her. But it had been an amazing and exhilarating experience (Chatterton, 2015).

'Communities' and processes of change: widening definitions and approaches?

Communities – however defined – can come together in response to threats of displacement and communities can be dispersed, whether as the result of violence or as the result of market pressures, or some combination of both. And communities can regroup, in the aftermath, whether locally or beyond, forming transnational communities in the process. They can come together to build intentional communities of solidarity and mutual support. And conversely, they can come together to build exclusionary barriers between themselves and the 'other', especially the 'others' from elsewhere.

People's community identifications can be varying, too, just as their identities can be multiple and changeable over time. So, for example, the writer Kamin Mohammadi reflected on the shifts in her own identifications as an exile, having fled from the violence associated with the Islamic Revolution in Iran. 'Growing up in Britain in the eighties, I had slipped on the mask of Englishness', she explained, 'denying Iran at every turn' (Mohammadi, 2011, p 211). 'I ran away from my parents' parties, from the tight community of Iranian friends', wanting to focus on her new life instead. 'Over the years', she continued, 'I became so good at wearing the mask that eventually, the mask became my face' (Mohammadi, 2011, p 211).

This was far from being the whole story, however, as the rest of the book goes on to explain, recounting the ways in which she came to discover her Iranian self, as a member of a community of Iranians – exiles who had spent their lives split between two places and cultures. 'Our culture and our history continues to enrich the souls of new Iranians born to families far from home', she concluded (Mohammadi,

2011, p 260), reflecting on the continuing complexities of people's identifications with places, identities, communities and cultures.

Anaheed Al-Hardan's study of Palestinian refugees in Syria tells a story of even more complexity (Al-Hardan, 2016). Palestinians fleeing the devastation and violence associated with the development of the state of Israel in 1948 formed a community when a group of them settled in Syria, but they were not homogeneous. There were differences relating to their varying places of origin in Palestine, along with differences relating to their places of residence in Syria and in terms of their economic class, just to name the most obvious. And there were differences that developed over time, both within and between Palestinian communities in Syria and elsewhere. Some became more economically integrated into Syrian society than others, for example, with greater opportunities in Syria compared with the more limited opportunities afforded to Palestinian refugees in other Arab countries. And there were variations in the extent to which Palestinian refugees in Syria identified as a diaspora community, and the extent of their commitment to the Right of Return to Palestine, variations that also shifted over time – until the devastation that forced these Palestinians to take refuge, once again, fleeing from the violence of civil war in Syria.

So communities are neither homogeneous nor fixed. Nor are they necessarily in conflict with each other – although they may be. And this applies to established working-class communities as well as to communities of newcomers in Britain (Beider, 2015).

But the potential for conflict can be all too easily exacerbated, whether deliberately manipulated (Hewitt, 2005) or unconsciously fuelled as the result of misguided policy interventions (Back, 1996), just as the potential for conflict can be fuelled by stereotypical portrayals of the 'other', neglecting to take account of the multifaceted ways in which people's identifications develop and change over time and space.

Hoque's study of third-generation Bangladeshi people in East London provides examples for illustration here (Hoque, 2015). The young Bangladeshi people in this study have already been referred to in the previous chapter in relation to the potential violence that they risked. In addition, they faced being labelled as potentially violent terrorists themselves, un–British and more generally 'other'. Typically, these young people wanted to reject such stereotypes – but not by retreating into the traditional ways of their parents' generation. Rather, they wanted to develop their own identities and senses of community, managing the complexities of being British, Bangladeshi and Muslim – with Islam as a central feature of their new, transnational sense of community. This, Hoque suggested, was how they negotiated their multiple identities, without being in conflict with what it means to be British.

Public policy-making needs to be based on understandings of such processes, including understandings of the range of issues *within* faith communities as well as *between* them (Dinham, 2009; Dinham et al, 2009; Report of the Commission on Religion and Belief in British Public Life, 2015). There needs to be understanding of the varying ways in which people's identifications develop over time and space, within and between communities of locality, interest and identity more generally. And most importantly, public policies need to address the structural disadvantages that fuel feelings of disaffection and conflict within and between communities as these feelings develop over time. The following chapter pursues these issues in further detail, exploring the implications for public policy at varying levels.

EIGHT

Public policies to promote community cohesion

Previous chapters have acknowledged 'community's' darker sides, although the previous chapter included community's warmer aspects, 'woven together from sharing and mutual care' (Bauman, 2001, p 150). This chapter focuses more specifically on ways of addressing 'community's' more exclusionary sides, and the conflicts of interest that can so easily be exacerbated *within* as well as *between* communities, however these are defined and managed – or not managed – via public policy processes. In recent times community cohesion has been an issue of concern for governments of varying political complexions. This has been in the context of widespread anxieties about the possible impacts of migration, coupled with widespread anxieties about the possibility of terrorist attacks.

Differing (mis)understandings of 'community' have underpinned a series of public policy interventions, along with differing perspectives on the nature of the underlying causes of the conflicts that need to be addressed. Was the focus to be on tackling attitudes and pathological behaviours within particular communities, as a number of critics have suggested (Kundnani, 2012)? Or was the approach to start from Bauman's wider concept of community, based on 'concern for the equal right to be human and the equal ability to act on that right' (Bauman, 2001, p 150)?

Having summarised the arguments, the chapter moves on to explore some of the ways in which public policy interventions can exacerbate conflicts within and between communities – even with the very best of intentions. Public policies can fail to take account of different interests, re-enforcing the power of the more powerful within communities, as previous chapters have suggested. Policy interventions can undermine trust within and between communities, just as they can have the effect of re-enforcing negative myths and stereotypes on all sides – 'suspect communities' of newcomers versus settled communities including settled communities of 'white working-class chavs'. They can obscure the underlying causes of grievances, including those arising from shared problems that could actually be tackled together, even across real or imagined community divides. And they can develop surveillance strategies that pose wider threats to civil liberties and basic human rights (McGhee, 2008; Kundnani, 2012).

The chapter concludes by focusing on examples of policy interventions that have been making a difference more constructively. These include examples of interventions that improve communication as well as those that address the underlying causes of tensions within and between communities. And they include policy interventions to support communities to identify shared concerns, negotiating differences between them while building social solidarity in the process.

Confusing concepts

The history of public policy interventions to address community conflicts goes back decades, if not far longer. From urban disturbances and predictions of 'rivers of blood' onwards, successive governments have launched a series of community interventions, turning to communities to address urban problems from the late 1960s (Wilks-Heeg, 2016). Aspects of such programmes have already emerged in the previous chapter, along with the accompanying criticisms. This chapter focuses on more recent interventions, addressing potential tensions arising from new patterns of migration, along with the fear of terrorism, post-2001. Before focusing on these interventions themselves, however, their underlying assumptions need to be unpacked. How were communities being conceptualised? And how was the notion of 'cohesion' being understood? Just as with the concept of 'community' itself, 'community cohesion' has been interpreted in varying ways, a policy catchphrase with differing implications in terms of policies and practices (Jones, 2013).

So, first, to return to the confusing concept of 'community' in the context of community cohesion policies, as Peter Ratcliffe and Ines Newman pointed out in their introduction to a collection of essays on the promotion of social cohesion, 'The notion of "community" has, of course, exercised the minds of social scientists for many decades' (2011, p 3) – with a tendency to be heavily ethnicised in the context of 'community cohesion' policy. Official publications commonly operationalised the term in ways that conflated communities of identity with 'the idea of "neighbourhood", in Ratcliffe and Newman's view, adding that neighbourhoods 'may, or may not, contain those from different "backgrounds"/ethnicities/faiths/social – class groups' (Ratcliffe and Newman, 2011, p 3). These were not mere pedantic quibbles, they emphasised. 'They are extremely important issues that go to the heart of policy, practice and the evaluation process.'

As Ratcliffe and Newman went on to point out, there was not only confusion surrounding the use of the term 'community'; there was confusion in terms of how this related to notions of cohesion, 'a failure to see cohesion as referring as much to intra- as to inter-group relations' (Ratcliffe and Newman, 2011, p 3). Failure to recognise such differences of interest within communities as well as between them could result in such difference being re-enforced. And this could include the re-enforcement of power differentials relating to age, ethnicity, gender, faith and social class, as the previous chapter has already argued.

In addition, Ratcliffe and Newman went on to identify the reverse side to this particular conceptual coin. Such confusion could obscure the potential scope for identifying genuinely common interests between communities, whether based on locality or identity. Communities were neither fixed nor necessarily in conflict with each other (Ratcliffe and Newman, 2011). On the contrary, in fact, communities could pursue common interests around the need for jobs with decent pay and conditions, for example, just as they could pursue shared interests around the need for affordable housing, access to education, health and welfare services, challenging existing patterns of inequalities within as well as between communities.

As Ratcliffe and Newman proceeded to conclude from this, community cohesion – broadly defined as being based on sustainable harmonious relationships – could only be achieved on the basis of a substantive reduction in material inequalities among those of different age/generation, gender and socioeconomic backgrounds, irrespective of ethnicity/faith/migrant status and so on (Ratcliffe and Newman, 2011), whereas the refusal to address, or even to recognise, the causes of people's grievances could serve to exacerbate feelings of alienation and the chances of social conflicts, with communities competing to meet their needs in the context of austerity policies more generally (McGhee, 2008; Kundnani, 2012; Jones, 2013).

Limited concepts of community can also be counter-productive in other ways. A focus on communities in terms of 'locality' risks losing sight of people's wider identifications, beyond the neighbourhood. And this includes migrants' identifications with their communities of origin, transnationally. This has been particularly contentious in the context of the War on Terror, with communities of newcomers being perceived as potentially, if not actually, suspect, especially if the newcomers in question happen to be Muslims. And this has been most especially marked if newcomers maintain their diasporic ties.

This is despite the evidence that enduring diasporic ties are neither incompatible with, nor binary opposite to, the development of more local identifications and engagements, as the previous chapter has already argued (Hickman et al, 2012). On the contrary, as Hoque concluded from his study of third-generation Bangladeshi people in East London, young people's identifications with the international Islamic community provided them with 'voice, visibility, belonging, representation and confidence to partake in the wider political process' (Hoque, 2015, p 3).

'I am proud to be Muslim', as one of those interviewed for this study emphasised (quoted in Hoque, 2015, p 93). This pride was only too understandably accompanied by feelings of frustration and anger, however, as a result of young people's experiences of discrimination. Reflecting on her arrival at the airport, for example, Zeyba explained that being taken aside to await the manager before she could be allowed through made her 'feel like, I don't know, a different species or something' (quoted in Hoque, 2015, p 95). But these feelings of frustration were in no way governed by a call to violent action. On the contrary, Hoque argued, it was 'membership of a symbolic Islam that affords them a sense of acceptance, recognition and makes them visible in the wider society' (Hoque, 2015, p 95).

As Hoque went on to suggest, British Islam is a dynamic identity, fluid, diverse, open to change and often contested by its members. Islam offers a sense of belonging to this third generation that neither fully belongs to a British nation nor to a Bangladeshi community. Zeyba described herself as belonging to 'one big family' of millions of Muslim brothers and sisters around the world (Hoque, 2015, p 102). And this sense of belonging to the transnational community of *Umma* was providing a sense of empowerment, enabling her to feel secure and confident as part of a greater Muslim whole.

Together, in Hoque's view, these third-generation Bangladeshi people had been generating a vibrant British-Islamic culture, with 'space to negotiate the many complex, overlapping and dynamic identities they are part of' (Hoque, 2011, p 112). As one of the girls explained, 'I am British because I was born here. But I am also so many other things – Bangladeshi, Muslim and a girl' (quoted in Hoque, 2011, p 119). These young people were finding their own ways forward, managing these different identities without necessarily seeing them as being in conflict with each other at all. 'Just because I am a Muslim, it doesn't mean that I cannot be British as well', Azad explained (quoted in Hoque, 2011, p 134).

The significance of diasporic ties emerges powerfully, too, through the story of the Abasindi black women's cooperative (Watt and Jones, 2015). As this account explains, the name 'Abasindi' – the Zulu word for 'survivors' – was chosen by members of the organisation that the women developed in the Manchester area from the 1960s. This name symbolised 'their tribute to the strength, resilience and competence of black women, in particular those in Africa and the African Diaspora that were actively involved in struggles against the dehumanizing and oppressive forces of apartheid, racism and sexism' (Watt and Jones, 2015, p 1). The aim was to provide a social support base for Black women, a community resource centre and, most importantly, educational and cultural activities, drawing on Black cultural traditions and creativity in Manchester and elsewhere, internationally.

Their focus on 'community' referenced the Civil Rights activist, Dr Martin Luther King Junior's, dream for 'a caring community where race and class was transcended' and social and economic justice 'the rule rather than the exception' (Watt and Jones, 2015, p 13). But 'while community can be a place for women's activism', they acknowledged that 'it can also be a place that limits women's control and choice' (Watt and Jones, 2015, p 25), hence the emphasis on providing space for development and growth. And hence the emphasis on the contributions of the arts, building on traditional art forms, story-telling as well as poetry, theatre, music and dance. By way of illustration, the Abasindi Cooperative's story includes accounts of the Abasindi drummers and dancers performances at two iconic festivals, one in Africa and one in the Caribbean.

The dancers built on traditional African dance forms, adapting them in the process to 'symbolize the role of Black women at the forefront of struggle within a specific socio-historical context, while at the same time passing on "culturally adumbrated" knowledge; or so we hoped' (quoted in Watt and Jones, 2015, p 73). 'We learned traditional African dances but danced them in our contemporary realities that for us, as women of the African and Caribbean Diaspora, were loaded with multiple, often contradictory, meanings' (quoted in Watt and Jones, 2015, p 75).

> Like drummers, we are masters of rhythm
>> Beating a time of yesterday
>> So that our spirits may soar tomorrow.
>>>>> (Watt and Jones, 2015, p 64)

These experiences of performing at international festivals were described as experiences of 'liberation and abandonment' (Watt and Jones, 2015, p 84). The Abasindi drumming and dance group was seen as a vehicle for rediscovering the value of their African and Caribbean cultural heritage, a journey that was historical, political and personal, through which 'we learned along the way'. 'The greatest beneficiaries', they concluded, were themselves. Far from diverting them from more local forms of community engagement and struggle, these transnational forms of cultural activism were associated with increasing feelings of empowerment. Abasindi women felt better able to confront racist ideologies, committed to supporting each other in their communities, continuing to fight for themselves and for the next generation of Black children in the UK.

What do policy-makers have in mind, in terms of promoting 'community cohesion'?

Diasporic cultural ties may have been empowering for Black women, reinforcing their involvement in their local communities in Britain, inspiring their commitment to equalities and social justice agendas. But this was hardly the focus of public policies to promote community cohesion. On the contrary, as already suggested, transnational connections have tended to be viewed with increasing suspicion.

So what, precisely, have policy-makers had in mind, in terms of 'cohesion' in general and 'community cohesion' more specifically? As Hannah Jones among others has pointed out, from 2001, following urban disturbances in the north of England, 'community cohesion' became a way of talking about issues of community, identity, belonging, connection and conflict. 'Discussion of community cohesion came to mean discussion of race equality, economic inequality, differences in beliefs, discrimination, tolerance and what role public authorities ought to have in each of these realms' (Jones, 2013, p 3). The disturbances themselves had involved groups of white men and British Asian men, for a number of reasons, including issues relating to drug dealing, it seemed. But public policy discourses came to focus far more specifically on concerns about tensions between different ethnic communities in these northern towns.

Multiculturalism was considered to have failed, re-enforcing differences between communities that were deemed to be leading parallel lives, as the report on the disturbances concluded (Cantle, 2001). Britain was seen to be sleepwalking into segregation, accompanied by the risk of increasing community conflicts as a result. This was a line of argument that could subsequently be pursued in particularly disturbing ways, with increasing concerns about fundamentalist terrorism. The Bishop of Rochester was quoted for his views on the connections between multiculturalism and the de facto segregation that was being re-enforced as a result, with people 'living as separate communities, continuing to communicate in their own languages and having minimum need for building healthy relationships with the majority' (quoted in Finney and Simpson, 2009, p 5).

In the context of a worldwide resurgence of 'the ideology of Islamic extremism', the Bishop continued, this was 'to further alienate the young from the nation in which they were growing up and also to turn already separate communities into "no-go" areas where adherence to this ideology has become a mark of acceptability' (quoted in Finney and Simpson, 2009, p 5). From multiculturalism to fundamentalist terrorism, in three easy stages? Critics have already pointed to the fallacies involved in these assumptions (Finney and Simpson, 2009; Kundnani, 2012), together with the ways in which they have diverted attention from alternative explanations, including explanations based on very different criticisms of multiculturalism.

Multiculturalism had been criticised for focusing on cultural aspects of difference – saris and samosas, for instance – at the expense of addressing more fundamental problems in the context of deindustrialisation. As Roger Hewitt's study of the white backlash demonstrated, this had to be understood against the background of factory closures and the consequent loss of jobs in South East London, the area of his research, along with what he described as 'a serious neglect of attention to the needs, legitimate wishes and feelings of white working-class communities' (Hewitt, 2005, p 29). As others have similarly pointed out, working-class communities have indeed expressed feelings of being unrepresented and unfairly treated, with multiculturalism being held to blame for their increasing feelings of marginalisation (Beider, 2015). 'My son can't get a job. But there are all these immigrants coming in and they're getting all the jobs. There are too many immigrants!', in the words of one of those canvassed during the 2010 General Election campaign in Britain, for example (Jones, 2011, p 221).

To add insult to injury, working-class communities have also been stigmatised for being particularly prone to racism. The term 'chavs' has been associated with such demonisation, writing off working-class anxieties as expressions of ignorance and prejudice, locating racism with the 'other' rather than addressing the underlying causes of people's concerns (Jones, 2011). As Lisa Mckenzie's study of the St Ann's Estate in Nottingham has similarly demonstrated, poor neighbourhoods have been blamed for society's ills, presented as objects of scorn (Mckenzie, 2015). As she argued on the basis of her research, however, the reality was more complex. There was also evidence of more positive realities, despite the social problems that were endemic on the estate. There were examples of people finding ways of getting by and supporting each other, for instance, just as there were examples of positive relationships across ethnic divides. As Beider has similarly concluded, there is not one working class, and white working-class people do not all blame immigration for their problems (Beider, 2015).

But politicians and public policy-makers can exacerbate the potential divisions that do exist, rather than promoting more inclusive approaches. Aggressive, moralistic anti-racism initiatives can actually make the situation even worse, as previous studies have demonstrated (Hewitt, 2005), silencing people rather than engaging with their multiple identifications or their common concerns (Back, 1996). And public policy interventions can backfire, even when policy-makers set out to intervene with the best of intentions. As Les Back's study of young lives in South East London housing estates back in the 1990s demonstrated, for example, young people could and did hold very different views simultaneously, with positive as well as negative attitudes towards the 'other'. And public policy interventions could have an impact on their views in varying ways – negatively as well as more positively.

Towards more 'cohesive communities'?

So how were these varying understandings being applied, in terms of public policy definitions and practices? At the start of the 21st century, a 'cohesive community' was described as being one where there was 'a common vision and sense of belonging', with respect for diversity and similar life opportunities for those of different backgrounds – linking integration and cohesion with equality of opportunity for all (LGA, 2002, p 6). The Commission on Integration and Cohesion's report that followed in 2007 took this approach further, setting out two interlocking principles, defining cohesion as 'principally the process that must happen in all communities to ensure that different groups of people get on well together; while integration is principally the process that ensures new residents and existing residents adapt to one another' (Commission on Integration and Cohesion, 2007, para e3.2). So the adaptation process was, in principle, to be a two-way street rather than the assimilation of newcomers into the local culture – however this might be defined. And newcomers' multiple identities were to be recognised and respected, including their transnational ties, which were portrayed as helping rather than hindering integration. A transnational identity 'may give people the confidence in their own identity to engage with the wider society', it was argued, rather than clashing with 'being part of the new society' (Commission on Integration and Cohesion, 2007, para 2.50).

The Commission on Integration and Cohesion went further, adding that the definition of an integrated and cohesive society should include that '(T)here is a strong sense of trust in institutions locally to act fairly in arbitrating between different interests and for their role and justifications to be subject to public scrutiny' (2007, para 3.15). This emphasis was based on the Commission's recognition that there were widespread concerns about the allocation of public services. Research for the Commission had demonstrated that over half of those interviewed felt that some groups in Britain were getting unfair priority in public services such as housing, health services and schools, while less than one in seven disagreed with this view. Public services needed to be allocated transparently as well as fairly, the Commission concluded, with commitments to equalities and social justice, if such suspicions were to be addressed – although dispelling such suspicions altogether has proved somewhat more challenging in practice.

Whatever the remaining limitations of official interventions to promote community cohesion – and the conceptual confusions that underpinned them in the first decade of the 21st century – these were still issues of public concern. Since then, however, under subsequent governments, the term has all but vanished from the public lexicon (Jones, 2013). Reflecting on the situation some 15 years after the publication of Ted Cantle's original report on the northern disturbances in 2001, the Labour MP Chuka Umunna pointed to this lack of attention to the promotion of community cohesion. While there were seemingly endless arguments about who should be let into the country, he suggested 'we pay scant attention to what happens when immigrants do pass through our borders and settle in our towns and cities' (Umunna, 2016, p 29). Making the case for action, he went on to point to the value of encouraging people to 'meet and mix and get to know one other', to enable trust to grow and communities to flourish. But this was only the first step, he continued. Governments should offer more support to communities to enable them to manage change, in his view, including investment in public services such as additional housing in migration hotspots (Umunna, 2016). This represented an alternative approach, implicitly challenging the neoliberal approaches that had come to predominate in public policy discourses.

As previous chapters have already outlined, neoliberal policies were geared towards reducing public spending, encouraging individuals to provide for themselves and their families via the private market, supplemented through voluntary and community initiatives and efforts. But this did not mean that the state had been disengaging from communities more generally. On the contrary, governments had been particularly – and increasingly – concerned to intervene in so-called 'suspect' communities, and to do so in ways that could end up by actually re-enforcing rather than challenging neoliberal policies overall.

Preventing violent extremism and/or reinforcing neoliberalism?

Preventing Violent Extremism (Prevent) agendas illustrate some of the ways in which community cohesion policies can backfire, together with some of the ways in which they can reinforce neoliberal policies more generally. The Prevent agenda was developed by the government of the day as part of the CONTEST strategy to tackle the causes of terrorist extremism in the wake of the 9/11 attacks in New York and the London bombings of 2005. These events raised real concerns. The question was not *whether* but *how* to address the causes of violent extremism, so how would these be addressed through the Prevent programme, setting out to 'win the hearts and minds of Muslims in our communities' (Commission on Integration and Cohesion, 2007, p 3)? Prevent began by issuing invitations to local authorities to submit bids for resources to support local initiatives to address these concerns within their communities.

The initiative was subject to criticisms right from the start. As Hannah Jones' study illustrates, based on her experiences as a policy officer in Hackney, London, at the time, Prevent was based on simplistic assumptions about communities as homogeneous entities. But this was far from being the case, Muslim communities in the area being ethnically diverse for a start. There were several different Muslim communities with varying interests and cultures in Hackney.

The focus on Muslims has been criticised for being limiting and discriminatory, failing to consider far right extremism. This aspect has been the subject of increasing concern with the rise of the far right in Europe (Fekete, 2014), along with the growth of hate crime in Britain, especially virulent since the referendum on membership of the EU in 2016.

And Prevent has been criticised for being potentially divisive, undermining relationships within as well as between communities, whether these were being defined in terms of locality or identity or both. In Hackney, for example, there were differences within and between communities right from the outset. Some groups were opposed to engaging with the programme at all, while others lobbied for the council to get involved so that they could access Prevent resources for their own particular projects (Jones, 2013).

Critics have also challenged other aspects of Prevent agenda's underlying assumptions. The focus has been on attitudes and individual religious beliefs and how these can be prevented from becoming radicalised. But this emphasis on ideology and faith has been limiting, diverting attention from underlying issues and grievances (Kundnani, 2012). This has been part of a wider shift of focus towards a harder-edged approach, with increasingly draconian anti-terrorism laws and decreasing emphasis on community relations and social justice concerns (McGhee, 2008). The effective denial of Muslim grievances has been antithetical, in McGhee's view, 'to the establishment of effective partnerships with Muslim communities in the war on extremism' (McGhee, 2008, p 51). And attempts to engage communities through local leaders have proved divisive, raising anxieties and potential suspicions that community spokespeople were becoming agents of surveillance, as the experiences of the SYRDC have already illustrated (see Chapter Three).

Failure to appreciate the complexities of communities and community identifications have also been factors, potentially undermining the effectiveness of Prevent. Critics have pointed to the initial focus on traditional community 'leaders', before appreciating that this was failing to engage younger men, let alone women and girls (McGhee, 2008). The failure to recognise the positive aspects of transnational identifications was similarly problematic, exacerbating rather than alleviating mutual suspicions, as the experiences of the young Somali men who visited Somaliland also illustrated.

Prevent agendas have become even more problematic in more recent times. Government policy was updated in 2011, maintaining Prevent as a key element of the government's approach to countering terrorism more generally. But the scope was to be widened. There has been increasing emphasis on targeting interventions more effectively, including targeting schools and universities as potential seedbeds of radical ideas. As critics of the Conservative government's legislative proposals pointed out in 2016, there were potential challenges and threats to be faced here. Academics were speaking out, for example, expressing concerns about the threat to freedom of speech and expression as a result of the government's 'extraordinarily intrusive and extraordinarily vague' anti-radicalisation legislation, risking 'sleepwalking into inequality and racial profiling' with the requirement on universities to report suspicions of radicalisation among their students and fellow academics (Wei and Ashworth, 2016). As a joint statement by academics and public figures (see http://www.preventwatch.org/joint-statement-on-prevent/) had already argued, reaffirming earlier criticisms, Prevent was based on 'an unsubstantiated view that religious ideology is the primary driving factor for terrorism', whereas academic research suggested that 'social, economic and political factors, as well as social exclusion plays a more central role in driving political violence than ideology'. Addressing these issues would be more effective, they concluded, whereas the Prevent agenda simply shifted attention away from the grievances that were driving individuals towards an ideology that was legitimising political violence.

There is not the space to go into debates on Prevent and its subsequent developments in further detail here. For the purposes of this chapter, the remaining point to be made is simply this, that anti-radicalism agendas in schools and other educational institutions have also fitted into wider agendas. In addition to the harmful effects on Muslim, black and minority ethnic youth, Sukarieh and Tannock have pointed out, for example, that there were negative effects in terms of the 'abandonment and undermining of the radical tradition in education', focusing on market-valued skills and knowledge at the expense of learning for social change (2015, p 24). The neoliberal state's retreat from the provision of public services was being offset by its expansion into the realms of mass surveillance (Kundnani, 2012).

Towards more promising practices?

So far the discussion has pointed to some of the limitations of public policy responses to the challenges of promoting community cohesion, however defined, together with some of the associated negativities and risks. But this is absolutely not to suggest that there have been no constructive achievements. On the contrary, as Chapter Six has already maintained, individuals and groups do have (at least some) agency. So do public policy-makers. And they can find ways of developing promising practices, even while taking account of wider constraints.

'Promising practices' was the term that we adopted, as a research team, back in the first decade of the 21st century, when we were exploring the challenges to be addressed if government policies to promote community engagement were to be genuinely inclusive of newcomers as well as involving more established communities (Blake et al, 2008). There were a number of implications to be identified from the three case studies of community engagement that we studied for this project.

These covered areas with differing experiences of migration and social change. Oldham was one of the northern towns that had been involved in the earlier disturbances, raising concerns about parallel lives (Cantle, 2001). Coventry, a city in the West Midlands, had differing histories of migration, with varying patterns of diversity. And Newham, an East London borough, had the highest levels of super-diversity and population churn in the country at that time. Given these variations, it was clear from the start that one size was not going to fit all as a model for good practice, hence the more tentative approach signalled by the use of the term 'promising practices'.

The questions that the research set out to address had emerged in the context of widespread concerns about rapid population change and super-diversity, with larger than anticipated flows of migrants from the Central and Eastern European Accession states. How were the newcomers' voices to be heard effectively via the structures that were being developed to promote decentralisation and community engagement – structures of governance such as Local Strategic Partnerships, set up to address community concerns, aiming to improve service delivery through community participation and empowerment? And most importantly, how was this to be achieved while taking account of the interests and concerns of established communities, including their anxieties as to whether newcomers were making additional demands on services that were already overstretched?

Previous studies had already demonstrated that newcomers were particularly at risk in terms of their wages and conditions, just as they were particularly at risk in terms of their housing situations (Spencer et al, 2007). Far from gaining preferential treatment, newcomers were experiencing additional disadvantages. But this was not necessarily how the situation was being perceived. On the contrary, previous research had already identified the role that deprivation and disadvantage were playing as factors in the ways in which new communities and established communities were relating to each other as they struggled to compete for more and more limited resources (Hudson et al, 2007; Spencer et al, 2007). The Commission for Integration and Cohesion's recommendations concerning the importance of transparency and accountability were particularly relevant here in terms of building understanding and trust between different communities – as well as building trust between communities and service providers more generally.

So how was the situation evolving in the context of policies to promote community participation and empowerment? Unsurprisingly, our research confirmed that there were, indeed, barriers for newcomers, inhibiting them from making their voices heard effectively in decentralised decision-making processes. A less anticipated finding was the extent to which their problems were being compounded by the complexity of the structures themselves, levels of complexity that were having an impact on newcomers and established communities alike. The research report included diagrams that resembled multiple spiders' webs rather than organisational charts, reflecting the fragmentation of decision-making that was accompanying decentralisation, compounded by increasing levels of outsourcing to alternative service providers (processes that have subsequently, of course, been increasing with further marketisation under different governments). This situation was confusing, even for well-established communities, but even more so for relatively new arrivals, adding to the challenges that they faced settling into an alien environment.

In addition, the research confirmed the importance of clarity in terms of defining communities and appreciating the differences within as well as between them. There were communities that were not being appropriately defined – or not even being formally defined as a community (such as the Kashmiri community in East London, for example, not officially recognised as a community at all, at the time, not having a recognised base in terms of its geographical origins). Other communities complained of being 'lumped together but fundamentally different, in how they migrated here, what facilities they want, what their family structures are', as a Black community worker pointed out, referring to the ways in which African and African Caribbean people were being (mis)categorised and consulted/or not consulted (quoted in Blake et al, 2008, p 32). Among South Asian people there were also major differences in terms of culture, religion, class, caste and political perspective, the report continued, not to forget differences in terms of age and gender. As a result, some voices were being ignored, leading to feelings of alienation and disempowerment.

Service providers may understandably prefer simplicity when categorising communities, enabling them to consult through identified spokespeople rather than engaging with the complexities of different interests within particular communities. As one of those interviewed for the research reflected, agencies may be comfortable with a 'tickbox' approach: 'they want a Somali representative to tick the Somali box, an Asian representative to tick the Asian box, but they are not interested in how they represent Somalis and Asians' (Blake et al, 2008, p 47). This type of approach proved to be problematic, however, as the research findings illustrated. So-called 'community leaders' were often elders, but what about the interests of young people and women, including young Muslim women? How were their views being represented? An alternative approach – being advocated by some of those entrusted with community engagement within the local authorities concerned – was to relate to informal networks as well as formal networks and groups, in order to reach beyond the usual community gatekeepers, so enabling other voices to be heard as well.

Decentralisation policies raised further questions. Communities based on neighbourhoods, such as tenants and residents' groups, could engage with locality-based structures of governance such as Neighbourhood Management Structures, taking up issues of service provision at this level. But this was more problematic for communities of interest. They could be geographically dispersed, across different neighbourhoods, and so less visible – and less effectively heard – in any particular neighbourhood management structure.

Or, as in the case of Oldham, the problem could be the reverse. As one of the champions of the town's inter-faith forum reflected, decentralised structures of governance were raising particular anxieties. The extent to which White British and Asian communities had been leading parallel lives had been the subject of concern. The extent to which this was actually the case had been the subject of some debate (Cantle, 2001; Finney and Simpson, 2009). But insofar as White British and Asian communities *were* each living in separate neighbourhoods, decentralisation policies could re-enforce this tendency, it was feared. Oldham's Youth Council had been seen as providing a safe space for young people from different communities to come together from across the town, to share common interests and concerns. But this could be undermined if the focus shifted towards neighbourhood-based structures and neighbourhood-based service provision, effectively re-enforcing rather than building bridges across community divides. Subsequent policies to promote localisation could pose further challenges still.

Focusing on the local level was seen as problematic in other ways, too. As a number of those interviewed pointed out, people's concerns were not confined to the neighbourhood level. On the contrary, issues such as those relating to asylum and immigration were beyond the remit of local government, involving decisions at central government level. These were issues of particular concern for newer communities.

But the limits of the local level also affected longer established communities. The research identified concerns about regional transport issues, for example, along with concerns about national policy issues such as pensions (understandably an issue of major concern for the pensioners' forums in these areas). Housing offered another example still, raising similar questions about the limits of community engagement with local authorities, given the impact of national policies, and the fragmentation of responsibilities for housing provision, processes of fragmentation that have subsequently been exacerbated, as already argued in previous chapters.

Despite identifying challenges, however, the research also identified a number of promising practices. These could be adapted and then applied to promote community cohesion and social solidarity more widely, taking account of the specifics of particular local circumstances. None of these could offer panaceas, of course, but they could illustrate ways in which local structures of governance could work in partnership with voluntary and community sector organisations to address their common concerns.

For instance, Coventry's New Communities Forum had been established with the support of the city's housing department officers, to reach out to new communities, contacting new arrivals and building links with a wide range of informal groupings and networks. As one of the officers involved reflected; 'if those working in formal structures of governance really want to reach new communities then they need to tap into these informal networks rather than waiting for new communities to come to them' (quoted in Blake et al, 2008, p 54). This inclusive approach brought some 80 community groups together when the forum was launched, building on the outreach and support work that had already been undertaken by a range of voluntary and community sector organisations, including the community development work that had been undertaken via the Coventry Refugee Centre. Meanwhile, the Coventry Voluntary Service Council had been providing support to strengthen Black and minority ethnic representation in local structures of governance more generally, as had the Multi-Faith Forum, which was similarly committed, aiming to 'help the excluded to be heard' as well as to 'help the institutions to listen' (Blake et al, 2008, p 56).

There were also examples of more informal cultural strategies to strengthen understanding between newer communities and longer-established communities, aiming to tackle misapprehensions and so improve mutual understandings as a result. Shared events, such as Newham's 'Under the Stars' programme of summer evening concerts, celebrated the cultural traditions of different communities in the borough. These events were evidently very popular, widely appreciated by newcomers and longer-established communities alike.

Festivals and sports events featured in other contexts, too, along with shared visits such as an annual day trip to the seaside organised with communities in one of the case study areas. As a resident representative commented, reflecting on one such event, 'you don't realise the effect on the community of that: getting 500 people together, talking with each other' possibly to some of their neighbours for the first time (quoted in Blake et al, 2008, p 62). As one of those interviewed also recognised, however, such events had to be carefully planned to take account of cultural differences. There were potentially sensitive issues around the consumption of alcohol, for instance, concerns that needed to be taken into consideration when planning the layout for cultural events.

Sensitivity was also essential when it came to planning myth-busting exercises. Previous research had identified potential problems such as the distribution of leaflets challenging myths about the negative effects of migration. Myths about the competition for housing against facts about the housing situation – such as the fact that migrants tended to live in the least desirable housing in the private rented sector, rather than jumping the queue for social housing – were problematic, it seemed. People could simply focus on the myths rather than the facts. They may not even be reading the facts themselves. And even if they did read them, they may not have believed them, especially if the leaflet in question came from an untrusted official source.

In one of the case study areas, this potential problem was being addressed by starting from identifying local people's particular fears. Having identified these fears, the myth-busting exercise focused on addressing these with the facts. These particular leaflets specifically avoided repeating the associated myths – thereby avoiding the risk of simply re-enforcing them.

Meanwhile there had been parallel efforts to work with the local media to discourage them from reproducing myths and negative stereotypes, let alone exacerbating tensions through sensational reporting. But attempts to work with the national media were apparently proving more difficult, to say the least.

While communication strategies featured significantly, there was recognition that these needed to be complemented with proactive strategies aimed at identifying and then addressing the symptoms of tension rapidly and effectively. In one case study area, for example, there were specific mechanisms for reporting racist graffiti, so that these could be speedily removed, just as there were mechanisms for dealing with hate crimes in timely and effective ways. Through such mechanisms trust could be developed, and the risks of conflict reduced for the future, officers believed.

Most importantly, the research also identified the potential significance of structures that brought local communities together to address their shared concerns. There were examples of varying types of joint forums, bringing voluntary and community sectors together, including faith-based organisations and inter-faith forums. Mosques, temples and churches were widely perceived as safe spaces where newcomers could receive advice and support, independently of official structures. In Oldham, for instance, an inter-faith forum had been established in 2002, following the disturbances of 2001. Since then a Women's Inter-Faith Network and a Young People's Inter-Faith Forum has also been established, to provide safe spaces for them to share their concerns as well, speaking for themselves directly rather than having their voices represented by others.

These developments were perceived as having contributed to bringing communities together in the face of common challenges, as one of those interviewed illustrated, by way of the example of community responses to the London bombings in 2005. Hundreds of residents had come together in Alexandra Park, Oldham, to express their solidarity, across community and faith divides.

Such forums could improve channels of communication between communities and structures of governance, but they needed to be supported, while retaining their independence from official structures. Voluntary and community-based organisations and groups needed resources in turn, if they were to undertake outreach work and provide community development support to others. This was a theme that emerged across the different case studies, leading to the recommendation that 'promising practices' depended on 'the development and implementation of community development strategies more generally' (Blake et al, 2008, p 71). Community development support was needed for the future sustainability of promising practices, working with established communities as well as newcomers, backed by local anchor organisations, umbrella bodies that were tackling racism and other forms of discrimination, solidarity within as well as between different communities, taking up issues of common concern.

These were no more than *potentially* promising practices, of course; they were certainly not being presented as magic bullets. But similar suggestions for public policy directions have emerged from other studies, too, including a European-level study in which I was also involved, along with colleagues from a number of European countries. The AMICALL project (Attitudes to Migrants, Communication and Local Leadership) was a transnational learning network to share and develop best practice among local and regional authorities in building public understanding of immigration and integration. This brought together local and regional government partners and researchers from six EU countries, the Netherlands and the UK with relatively long histories of migration, together with Germany, Hungary, Italy and Spain, with relatively more recent increases in migratory flows. While recognising the differences between these contexts, the aim was to share learning about good practices, especially focusing on communication strategies to promote integration and cohesion. Our task, as one of a number of teams of researchers within AMICALL, was to evaluate the added value of the transnational aspects of the programme, rather than focusing on the research findings from each national context per se (Mayo and Rooke, 2012). But we did identify examples of outcomes that were emerging from promising practices as part this evaluation process, since these examples were being shared transnationally.

For the concerns of this particular chapter, the most relevant examples of transnational learning included exchanges around anti-rumour initiatives. As previous research had already demonstrated – and been taken into account in the case studies that we had previously studied – simply setting the 'facts' alongside the myths and the rumours could be counter-productive. In Barcelona, Spain, for instance, far more imaginative approaches were being adopted. These involved working through local activists, briefing them, and then supporting them to challenge the prevalent rumours and myths, local activists being far more likely to be trusted and believed than local officials. AMICALL partners from elsewhere were interested in applying this type of approach in their own national contexts.

There were a number of examples of strategies that involved celebratory community events, such as a festival in a German city based around opportunities for sharing food from different cultures. And there were examples of community development support being provided to enable different communities to take up shared concerns together at the neighbourhood level. Planning and redevelopment issues presented challenges for newcomers and longer-established residents alike in an Italian context, for instance, offering opportunities for the development of common strategies in response.

Most importantly there were lessons to be learned in terms of the ways in which different local and regional authorities engaged with different communities and evaluated the impact of their strategies as a result. Despite efforts by the programme organisers, civil society representation in AMICALL itself had been too limited, AMICALL partners also concluded. And this absence was particularly marked in relation to migrant organisations and communities. Overall, migrant organisations had made up 7% of roundtable participants compared with 61% from local and regional authorities.

The AMICALL project was completed in 2012, providing evidence of transnational learning about varying ways of promoting community cohesion – despite the challenges – including the challenges for evaluative research across differing national contexts. But policy developments have been moving in very different directions, in more recent times, and especially so in Britain, with increasing concerns about immigration, together with mounting anxieties about the refugee crisis, coupled with growing concerns about terrorism (including concerns that Islamic terrorists might be entering the country, masquerading as refugees from the war in Syria). This is the framework within which local strategies to promote community cohesion have to operate in the contemporary context.

In summary

To summarise the argument so far, public policies can make a difference at the local level. Local and regional authorities can work alongside communities to promote greater understanding, taking account of the differences within as well as between them. Politicians can take a lead, promoting agendas based on mutual respect. And they can support communities to address their common concerns, building solidarity through the process of working together for their mutual benefit. But public policy interventions to promote community cohesion can backfire, even with the best of intentions. And public policy interventions can exacerbate conflicts within and between communities, evading rather than addressing the underlying causes of communities' concerns. These underlying causes need to be identified and addressed at the relevant policy levels.

This takes the discussion back to the example of the SYDRC's concerns about increasing instances of school exclusions and declining levels of educational attainment within their community in north London. Was this due to problems within the school system, or were there contributory factors to be taken into account as well? Were parents working longer and more irregular hours on precarious zero hours contracts, leaving less time to encourage their children to study?

Was the housing crisis affecting young people's education, with frequent moves from one insecure tenancy to another, and longer journeys to school as a result? One of those interviewed for this study was Amina, the mother who had been supported with her housing problems (see Chapter Five). Since I had met with her previously she had been forced to move once more and was currently facing the threat of eviction, yet again. Unsurprisingly, the housing situation had been affecting her son's performance at school, she explained.

What about wider pressures? Girls had been expressing concerns about the discrimination and abuse that was associated with the wearing of headscarves – including examples of girls having had their headscarves torn off. And what about fears of bullying, violence and increasing alienation among young people more generally, as a result of Prevent, not to forget the impact of British foreign policy interventions over the longer term? These are issues that are still being explored, at the time of writing.

Without minimising the problems, there was emerging evidence that some schools had been developing extremely effective ways of supporting young people, despite these wider pressures. There were lessons to be shared more widely. The local authority was committed to ensuring that good practices were to be developed across the borough, taking account of community concerns, building more effective ways of communicating with parents and young people from differing communities across the area.

In terms of local policy developments SYDRC's approach has been cited as a model by the local authority involved, demonstrating ways in which local authorities can work alongside communities to improve service delivery and widen access for the future. Both SYDRC and the local authority in question have been keen to develop approaches that can be applied to the needs of other communities, too, including white working-class communities, where boys' problems with under-achievement have been raising similar questions. As previous chapters have already argued, people do have agency and so do policy-makers. Local authorities can choose to work in partnership with local communities to address their common concerns, sharing lessons in ways that promote social solidarity and cohesion rather than exacerbating competition and conflicts.

But the limits of local policy interventions emerge only too clearly. There are national issues of educational policy involved, just as there are wider policy issues relating to employment/precarious employment, inadequate training opportunities and social welfare benefit reforms/cuts, along with housing and planning policies and social cleansing, just to identify the most obvious. And there are issues with wider, international ramifications, including the continuing impacts of British foreign policy and the War on Terror, not to forget the growth of populist movements on the far right of the political spectrum.

These are issues that have an impact on communities in varying ways, but there are common threads having an impact on newcomers and longer-established communities alike. The following chapter explores a number of the implications for developing common understandings among those working with communities, whether as front-line professionals or unpaid community activists, providing the basis for building wider alliances in the pursuit of social justice agendas.

NINE

Moving on?

There is a crack in everything. That's how the light gets in.
(Leonard Cohen, 1934–2016)

This book started from contemporary concerns with migration, displacement and dispossession on unprecedented scales, whether people have been moving as the result of violence, ethnic cleansing or natural disasters, or in search of better livelihoods and security for themselves and their families. Others have been moving as the result of processes of 'social cleansing', displacement by market forces, especially when have been being re-enforced, rather than challenged, by urban policy interventions. There are underlying structural factors to be addressed here, in the context of neoliberal globalisation, with increasing inequalities of wealth and power, accompanied by increasing anxieties about violence and international terrorism.

As the opening chapter also identified, there are issues to be addressed within and between communities. Communities can, and too often do, exacerbate the effects of displacement, becoming fragmented and divided in the process, blaming each other/the 'other' for their frustrations and anxieties. But these are so far from being the only options, as previous chapters have also demonstrated. Alternatives approaches can be, and are being, developed, as part of wider strategies for the promotion of social solidarity and social justice.

This is absolutely not to conclude by proposing any particular blueprint or blueprints for the future. On the contrary – one size most clearly won't fit all. Rather, the conclusions will simply refer back to some of the more promising practices that have been emerging from previous chapters, identifying some of the ways that communities can move on, building and rebuilding themselves in less socially divisive ways, developing mutual supports and social solidarities, at both local and transnational levels. What common understandings might be useful here? How might such understandings be convincingly shared more widely? How might these contribute to the development of effective alliances to promote social justice agendas? And how might the arts contribute to increasing mutual understanding and empathy, contributing to the development of movements for social change?

Developing common understandings of communities and change in the global context

Just as people can have multiple identities, so can they identify with multiple communities. As Amartya Sen has already pointed out (2006), there is no need to suggest that our national allegiances and local loyalties should be replaced by a global sense of belonging, or vice versa. 'We do belong to many different groups, in one way or another, and each of these collectivities can give a person a potentially important identity' (Sen, 2006, p 24). People can and do belong to communities of identity as well as to communities based on shared interests, just as they can and do belong to communities of locality within their neighbourhoods while continuing to maintain transnational ties as part of diasporic communities. Communities form and reconstitute themselves, over time and space, just as the strength of people's attachments to such communities can vary, depending on the social contexts in question. Boxing people into the confines of any one particular category fails to take account of these complexities. And this risks defining communities in mutually exclusive ways, separating people out, describing whole communities divisively in terms of 'us' – and 'them'. The more I think about the challenges of promoting solidarity in the context of globalisation, the more crucial such understandings would seem to be, starting from people's interests in common while respecting their continuing attachments elsewhere.

This links with the need for communities and those that work with them to share common understandings of the interconnections between the global and the local more generally. There are implications here when it comes to developing strategies for change, strategies that take account of the structures of power and the levels at which to address these most effectively. Local community strategies can re-enforce rather than distract from strategies for change at the national level and beyond, just as addressing people's immediate needs can contribute to, rather than distract from, the development of strategies to address the underlying causes of their problems. These do not have to involve 'either/or' choices about zero sum gains, to state the blindingly obvious, whatever may have been implied by critics of particular community intervention programmes in the past (Fisher and Dimberg, 2016).

The Global Campaign for Education (GCE) (see www.campaignforeducation.org/en/) provided evidence to illustrate these interconnections, links that I was able to record myself, when I had the opportunity to take part in research with John Gaventa (Gaventa and Mayo, 2010). This particular piece of research was part of a wider series of international projects, exploring the interrelationships between the local and the global, and their consequences for the identities of citizenship and the practices of active citizenship (Gaventa and Tandon, 2010). Although the focus of this particular research related to debates on aspects of international development, the findings about the links between the local and the global have wider relevance.

As one of those campaigning for the right to quality, free education for all, reflected,

> Now anything which is just local is not going to solve the problem [that is, the problem of the lack of resources for schooling, especially in the poorest contexts in the global South].... The sites of authority and power have changed ... [and] when the sites of authority and power have changed, the sites of struggle will have to be changed ... it means being local, it also means being global. (Gaventa and Mayo, 2010, p 146)

Local campaigners needed to ensure that resources were being spent effectively – and that parents were actually sending their children to school (school drop-out being a particular issue for girls in the contexts that we studied, in India and Nigeria). National campaigners needed to keep up the pressure at national government levels. And international campaigners needed to keep up the pressure for resources from international agencies.

Of course there could be tensions, despite such common understandings of the potential links between different levels of action. Local campaigners could be made to feel like second-class citizens, for example, welcomed as sources of information and legitimisation but not treated as equals by those who were jetting across continents to make the case on their behalf. Who speaks for whom, whether at local, national or international levels? But coalitions could be developed in more mutually beneficial ways, given the time and space – and most importantly, the commitment – to build the necessary trust.

The GCE's guide for practitioners and activists working on education rights emphasised the importance of developing such degrees of understanding and trust, working across different levels 'with clear roles and space for all to play to their strengths'. There needed to be recognition of 'the different knowledge and skills that each person or organisation brings', the guide continued, emphasising the need for 'collaboration, not competition, and a constant awareness of and strategies to minimise potential conflicts and unequal power relations'

(GCE, 2007, p 11). These conclusions could equally apply to the processes of building transnational alliances more generally. As previous chapters have already argued, the underlying causes of displacement need to be addressed, as well as the more immediate impacts. And this involves building transnational coalitions with anti-war movements and movements campaigning against the use of weapons of mass destruction, along with human rights organisations, just as this involves engaging with more local groups working with migrants, refugees and asylum-seekers and other potentially vulnerable groups.

Linking the personal and the political

There also needs to be recognition of the potential links between the personal and the political, supporting people to address their individual needs while campaigning to address the underlying causes of their problems. These could be seen to be in conflict with each other, as project aims, but they can actually be combined in mutually reinforcing ways, as previous chapters have already suggested.

The documentary DVD 'Si se puede' ('Yes we can') provides further illustration, focusing on the citizens' Platform for People Affected by Mortgages movement in Barcelona (Plataforma de Afectados por la Hipoteca, PAH) following the crash in the housing market in Spain. The DVD tracks the movement's activities over a seven-day period, in February 2014, supporting those resisting evictions, providing physical and emotional support for those affected and vigorously campaigning, sharing understandings about the causes of displacement and dispossession in the first place, empowering those involved in the community in the process. As C. Wright Mills had earlier commented, reflecting on the potential contributions of sociology more generally, the sociological imagination could enable what might seem to be 'private troubles' to be understood as 'public issues', to be tackled in their wider socioeconomic and political contexts (Mills, 1959).

This particular DVD starts from the eviction of a family with three children, interspersing this story and other people's stories with explanations of the underlying causes of their problems. As a result of market failures, Spain was in the absurd position of having become a country with many empty dwellings but many evictions.

On Mondays the organisation provided advice and support to individuals facing the threat of eviction, and, as if this wasn't problematic enough, it was typically associated with feelings of stigmatisation and guilt. "People who have lost everything have [been made] to feel ashamed of being poor", one of the organisers explained, whereas they were telling people the opposite: "Don't feel guilty … become empowered and informed … you won't be alone." People were being supported to take up their own cases, and then to support others in their turn.

On Wednesdays, the mutual support group met. People came to share their feelings, giving the meeting a more emotional focus. As one of those interviewed for the DVD recounted, these meetings, together with her husband's continuing support, were more effective than the anti-depressants that she had been proscribed for her depression in the face of eviction. "I've learned to share my feelings" in the group, she explained.

Meanwhile, on subsequent days, the Coordination Assembly focused on campaigning, developing strategies, moving from negotiation tactics through to varying forms of non-violent civil disobedience. Negotiating with banks that were planning evictions involved strategic planning, for instance, challenging some basic assumptions in the process. "They talk about money. I talk about people", as one of the negotiators explained. If negotiations failed to produce results, direct action could follow. For example, a bank that refused to negotiate had been occupied by a group of activists, dancing flamenco with gusto, thereby ensuring that no work could be done in that office that day. Another example of direct action involved the occupation of empty flats, to provide homes for those who had been evicted. The DVD showed the activists making communal gardens on the occupied roof terraces, growing vegetables to provide healthy, affordable meals for the new residents.

These experiences illustrate the need for shared understanding here, recognising that the 'private troubles' of evictions need to be addressed as 'public issues' too. And they demonstrate the importance of shared learning as the basis for building solidarity, enabling people to support each other as part of a nationally coordinated movement for change. The challenges involved in moving in such directions have been continuing themes throughout this book.

People have too often been labelled in ways that have stigmatised and disempowered them. And they have too often been defined in terms of categories that have had divisive effects. The displaced have had to contend with these processes of categorisation and labelling, whether they have been dispossessed as the result of disastrous failures in housing markets, compounded by disastrous failures of urban policy, or whether they have moved across borders as migrants or refugees. Refugees have generally been labelled more positively than migrants, even if there have been overlapping reasons for their moves. And migrants have been popularly distinguished from each other – implicitly, if not explicitly – depending on their race, religion, social class and educational level.

The point to emphasise here is simply this, that communities need to share more nuanced understandings of the varying factors involved in people's decisions to migrate, taking account of their differing circumstances as well as of the extent to which they have, or have not, been able to exercise choice in the process. Without such shared understanding it is all too easy for some newcomers – if not necessarily all newcomers – to be defined and stereotyped as the 'other', with varying implications, depending on their socioeconomic situations, along with their gender, age, ethnicity and faith. And similarly, in parallel, it has been all too easy for those displaced from within the city to be popularly perceived as homeless scroungers, rather than having their 'private troubles' perceived as being the 'public' and political issues that they really are. 'There is no "them and us" – just us', John Hills has so persuasively argued in the context of debates on the welfare state more generally (Hills, 2015, p 266).

But how can we develop such shared learning and mutual understanding as the basis for building social solidarity in action?

Sharing understandings – convincingly?

One conclusion that would seem to have been emerging with particular clarity from previous chapters is this, that giving people the 'facts', telling them the 'right' answers, simply doesn't work. On the contrary, this can actually be counterproductive. The facts do not speak for themselves, even if there is general agreement about the facts in question. And this is typically not the case, especially when it comes to considering such contentious issues as migration and displacement – for whatever reasons, in whichever contexts.

As Amartya Sen has argued more generally, there has been an assumption among many modern economists that individuals make decisions on the basis of narrowly defined self-interest. The implications for the study of migration, displacement and dispossession have already been explored in previous chapters. As Sen has characterised this approach, '(T)he single-minded self-loving human being, who provides the behavioural foundations of a great many economic theories, has been adorned often enough by elevating nomenclature, such as being called "economic man" or "the rational agent"' (Sen, 2006, p 22). Despite critiques of this 'presumption of single-mindedly self-seeking economic behaviour', he continued, much modern economic theory has 'tended to proceed as if these doubts were of marginal concern and could be easily brushed off' (Sen, 2006, p 23) – at least until more recently, as further evidence has been emerging, in his view, identifying the significance of a range of other influences affecting individual decision-making.

The role of emotions has already been identified as having major impacts on people's perceptions and behaviours, emotions of fear and resentment having particular relevance in terms of understanding negative responses to the 'other' (Hoggett et al, 2013). As previous chapters have also suggested, such emotions can be all too easily magnified by politicians and amplified by the media, as the 2016 referendum campaign to persuade voters that Britain should leave the EU so amply demonstrated. The ensuing growth of hate crime has been all too predictable, given the negativity of xenophobic campaigning involved.

So presenting people with the facts isn't necessarily going to change their minds, let alone change their behaviours. And myth-busting exercises can actually backfire, as has already been suggested, re-enforcing people's prejudices, further alienating them from the myth-busters in the process, fuelling their distrust of decision-makers, especially politicians, more generally. People are more likely to be influenced by those they trust, especially people from within their own communities.

Previous chapters have also pointed to the roles that the arts can play, engaging with people's emotions rather than simply appealing to them with the 'facts'. Community festivals can bring people together. Drama can enable people to rethink their situations, exploring the possibility for alternative ways of acting, as the work of Augusto Boal has demonstrated (Boal, 1979). The use of photographs and poems can enrich people's activism, as the experiences of the Abasindi Cooperative illustrated in Chapter Eight (Watt and Jones, 2015). And music and song can express emotions in ways that build mutual support and social solidarity within and between communities.

There would seem to be a number of implications for community education and development workers here, along with potential implications for the organisations that train them and the agencies that employ them. Previous chapters have already provided illustrations of the ways in which communities have learned together, sharing expertise and skills as they reflected on the implications of their experiences. People can and do succeed in doing it for themselves – including through engaging in community arts. But this is not invariably the case. Communities can and do also value support from outside, whether this comes from other communities, engaged in similar issues elsewhere, or from those with relevant professional expertise, as the experiences of housing activists in London demonstrated, for example.

A number of sources have already been quoted in previous chapters making the case for continuing resources for community education and development, including community arts (Kenny et al, 2015; Fisher and Dimberg, 2016). Whatever the inherent limitations of officially sponsored community interventions, they can actually increase the chances of people organising in opposition to politics and policies that exacerbate discrimination and disadvantage, in Fisher and Dimberg's view (2016). And conversely, without such support, some of the most vulnerable run the risk of experiencing still further disadvantages, losing out in terms of their life chances, and out in terms of their access to much needed public services as well as in terms of the resources to make their voices heard most effectively.

The importance of civic infrastructures emerges with particular clarity from Jane Wills' research on popular initiatives to promote localism (Wills, 2016). Her study starts from the widening gap between people and politicians, focusing on bottom-up rather than top-down policy responses to this challenge, exploring ways of shifting power more equitably downwards to the local level. She draws on her own experiences too, providing examples of communities mobilising alongside faith-based organisations and trade unions, building coalitions within their localities in East London and elsewhere, taking up issues of particular concern for migrants and refugees, such as poverty pay and poor employment conditions, issues that have been problematic for longer-established communities too. The London Campaign for a Living Wage has been a case in point, demonstrating the potential for achieving significant gains as a result.

But even here, despite their successes, organising around issues such as low pay and precarious employment, the community-based organisations that formed the basis for the membership of the London Campaign for a Living Wage were actually feeling pressured themselves. Many groups were described as 'struggling to secure their own organisations, let alone being able to reach out to others in a broader alliance' (Wills, 2016, p 189). So efforts to create 'a more permanent infrastructure at the neighbourhood scale will prove critical', Jane Wills concluded, making the case for providing community development support structures more generally (Wills, 2016, p 207).

The case of the GCE provides evidence to re-enforce this conclusion, the importance of providing resources to support community-based mobilisations emerging as being even more crucial at national and international levels. How else could representatives afford to travel to meetings elsewhere within their own countries, for example, let alone participate in meetings and mobilisations involving travel further afield? Communities need access to resources, whether this involves material forms of support or particular forms of expertise, to facilitate the development of shared understanding and effective strategies for change – or both. And this applies both locally and beyond (Gaventa and Mayo, 2010).

Developing alliances across differences of organisational culture and style

Before moving on to conclude with the potential roles that the arts can play, promoting critical thinking and shared feelings as well as shared understanding, developing empathy across differences, I include a brief digression on some of the challenges involved in building alliances for social change.

Building alliances is potentially problematic per se, especially when it comes to developing mutually re-enforcing connections between the local and the global. Previous chapters have also reflected on some of the issues to be addressed – how to work across differences within as well as between communities, identifying underlying interests in common? How to construct alliances on a limited basis, even across such differences? And how to recognise when differences of interest have more fundamental bases? These are centrally important questions for those committed to developing strategies to promote social solidarity as part of wider agendas for equalities and social justice.

There are additional challenges to be faced, too, when it comes to building alliances across differences of organisational culture and style. Communities organise in varying ways. And so do their potential allies, such as trade unions. There are, of course, differences within and between trade unions at different levels, locally, regionally, nationally and internationally. But typically trade unions organise in a 'vertical' style, meaning that they have relatively hierarchical decision-making structures with representatives selected via formal electoral processes. Democratic accountability is clear for all to see, in principle (even if considerable power can become concentrated at the centre, in practice).

Communities and social movements, including global justice movements, are often more 'horizontal' in style, opting for more fluid organisational forms (Della Porta and Rucht, 2013). Decisions may be made via open general assemblies, for example. And leadership styles may be more collective – even if less clearly accountable. There are potential tensions between these different organisational approaches, requiring mutual understanding for the development of trust.

A study of the already mentioned London Campaign for a Living Wage (Holgate, 2009) provides an example for illustration here. Many of those in the relevant community organisations perceived the trade unions as being overly bureaucratic and slow (Holgate, 2009). Trade unions were caricatured as 'pale, male and stale' (Mayo et al, 2016) – and so incapable of responding rapidly as the campaign developed – while the trade unions perceived the community organisation in question as being fundamentally undemocratic in its ways of operating, not recognising its annual open assemblies as proper democratic structures at all. These misconceptions and stereotypes had to be addressed, along with the cultural differences within and between communities and faith groups in the area, campaigning together for a living wage for migrants and longer established communities alike, building mutual respect for very different traditions, cultures and organisational styles.

Despite the challenges, the need for such alliances has been increasingly evident, in the context of austerity, the further marketisation of public services and the increasingly precarious nature of jobs, including public service jobs. As a result, community unionism has been developing in a number of contexts internationally, including Australia, Canada and the US. And here, too, there has been shared learning from these varying experiences (Holgate, 2015). These types of alliances have been centrally important in terms of building social movements to address the causes of displacement and dispossession, effectively pursuing social and environmental justice for the longer term while complementing the ways in which communities have been organising to meet the most immediate needs, in the here and now.

Community arts and social change

Previous chapters have illustrated varying ways in which the arts have been contributing to shared understandings and empathy, within and between communities. People have found ways of expressing their feelings through song and dance, just as they have found ways of sharing these feelings with wider audiences through creative writing. The arts can provide the stimulus to question accepted ways of thinking, within and between communities, whether such questioning leads to increased understanding and empathy – or not. Such questioning can contribute to processes of social change.

The obituary for historian and biographer Alex Danchev included reflections on his views on this aspect of the power of art. 'Armed with art … we are more alert and less deceived', Alex Danchev had maintained (Cowling, 2016, p 37). As Seamus Heaney had similarly argued, 'The imaginative transformation of human life is the means by which we can most truly grasp and comprehend it' (quoted in Cowling, 2016). This enabled artists to contribute to the creation of a new world order, in Alex Danchev's view.

More specifically, the musician, Daniel Barenboim, has written of the power of music to enable people to listen to one another, promoting the processes of dialogue and reciprocal understanding that he describes as 'the very foundation of humanity' (Barenboim, 2016, p 39). On the day that Daniel B was writing, the West-Eastern Divan orchestra (so named after a collection of Goethe's poetry) was bringing musicians together across the divides between Israel and its Arab neighbours, celebrating Human Rights Day with a concert in Geneva. As Barenboim went on to explain, 'In our orchestra, diversity is lived on a daily basis and no musician can exist without a fundamental appreciation of the other, however different.' This orchestra had grown into what he described as 'an example of how society could function…. Our musicians have gone through the painful process of learning to express themselves while listening to the narrative of their counterparts', he added. 'I cannot imagine a better way of implementing the first and most fundamental article of the UN Declaration of Human Rights: that all human beings are born free and equal, and should act towards one another in a spirit of brotherhood.' Music could make this possible as a 'constant, simultaneous conversation between apparent opposites that can peacefully exist side by side' (Barenboim, 2016, p 39).

The arts can also celebrate people's cultures and achievements. This celebratory aspect emerged most powerfully on a visit I made to the Turner Contemporary art gallery in Margate in 2016. The plan for the day had been very different, as it happened. I was on the way to Dover with others as part of a convoy of 250 or so vehicles, taking supplies to the refugees encamped in the Calais 'Jungle' across the Channel. We were going to express our solidarity, as well as provide more practical forms of support – like food. But just as we reached Dover it emerged that the convoy was not going to be allowed to pass. Vehicles were being 'kettled' (that is, held in a cordon) at the entrance to the port. Fortunately some of the supplies had already got through, by another route, but we were stuck.

So a small group of us decided to proceed to Margate to see the Turner Contemporary gallery instead. And there we found an extraordinary exhibition, displaying the work of a leading contemporary artist, Yinka Shonibare. The exhibit that I found most particularly compelling was entitled 'The British library'. This was described in the accompanying leaflet as:

> … a colourful work, celebrating and questioning how immigration has contributed to the British culture that we live in today. Shelves of books covered in colourful wax fabric fill the Sunley Gallery, their spines bearing the names of immigrants who have enriched British society. From T.S. Eliot [poet] and Hans Holbein [painter] to Zaha Hadid [architect], 'The British library' reminds us that the displacement of communities by global war has consequences that inform our lives and attitudes today.…

The entire Sunley Gallery was filled with these shelves, full of staggeringly beautiful books, bound with the gorgeous wax fabrics that resonated with Yinka Shonibare's own West African heritage. Faced with this extraordinary evidence of talent, how could the contribution of immigration to British culture be in doubt? But of course it could. Was there perhaps a certain irony to the day's excursions?

Yinka Shonibare's exhibition represented the creativity of a leading artist, stimulating his audiences to question while enjoying the visual beauty of his work. But creativity is not, of course, confined to those producing works of international renown. As previous chapters have already pointed out, people can and do engage in the arts in their communities too, whether these are communities of locality or of interest, both locally and transnationally, sharing their emotions and expressing solidarity in the face of displacement and dispossession.

The Family Care Group's collaborative poem, written together by migrant, asylum-seeker and refugee women, for International Women's Day 2015:

> When we're sad we're sad together
> When we are worried we are worried together
> When we're happy we're happy together
> When we dance we dance together
> When we eat we eat together
> When we joke we joke together
> When we sing we sing together
> We are all together, we are one.

References

Achebe, C. (2012) *There was a country: A personal history of Biafra*, London: Penguin.

Adiche, C.N. (2007) *Half of a yellow sun*, London: Harper.

Adiga, A. (2011) *Last man in tower*, London: Atlantic.

Al-Hardan, A. (2016) *Palestinians in Syria*, New York: Columbia University Press.

Back, L. (1996) *New ethnicities and urban cultures*, London: UCL Press.

Barenboim, D. (2016) 'Our rights won't be protected by tolerance alone', *The Guardian,* 10 December.

Basch, L., Glick Schiller, N. and Blanc, C.S. (1993) *Nations unbound: Transnational projects, postcolonial predicaments and deterritorialized nation-states*, London: Routledge.

Batnitzky, A. and McDowell, L. (2013) 'The emergence of an ethnic economy?', *Ethnic and Racial Studies*, vol 36, no 12, pp 1997-2015.

Bauman, Z. (1998) *Globalization: The human consequences*, Cambridge: Polity Press.

Bauman, Z. (2001) *Community: Seeking safety in an insecure world*, Cambridge: Polity Press.

Beazley, M., Loftman, P. and Nevin, B. (1997) 'Downtown redevelopment and community resistance: An international perspective', in N. Jewison and S. Macgregor (eds) *Transforming cities: New spatial divisions and social transformation,* London: Routledge, pp 181-92.

Beider, H. (2015) *White working-class voices: Multiculturalism, community-building and change*, Bristol: Policy Press.

Berger, J. and Mohr, J. (2010) *A seventh man: Migrant workers in Europe*, London: Verso.

Blake, G., Diamond, J., Foot, J., Gidley, B., Mayo, M., Shukra, K. and Yarnit, M. (2008) *Community engagement and community cohesion*, York: Joseph Rowntree Foundation.

Boal, A. (1979) *Theatre of the oppressed*, London: Pluto.

Boal, A. (1995) *The rainbow of desire*, London: Routledge.

Boal, A. (1998) *Legislative theatre*, London: Routledge.

Booth, R. (2015) 'New Era estate could means-test residents to set individual rents', *The Guardian*, 25 February.

Bourdieu, P. (2003) *Outline of a theory of practice*, Cambridge: Cambridge University Press.

Branson, N. (ed) (1984) 'Squatters 1946', Proceedings of a conference held by the Communist Party History Group, May.

Brenner, N., Marcuse, P. and Mayer, M. (eds) (2012) *Cities for people, not for profit: Critical urban theory and the right to the city*, London: Routledge.

Burra, S. (1999) *Resettlement and rehabilitation of the urban poor: The story of Kanjur Marg*, Mumbai, India: SPARC (Society for the Promotion of Area Resource Centers).

Cantle, T. (2001) *Community cohesion: A report of the Independent Review Team chaired by Ted Cantle*, London: Home Office.

Castles, S. and Miller, M. (2003) *The age of migration: International population movements in the modern world* (3rd edn), Basingstoke: Palgrave Macmillan.

Castles, S., de Haas, H. and Miller, M. (2014) *The age of migration: International population movements in the modern world* (5th edn), Basingstoke: Palgrave Macmillan.

Chatterton, P. (2015) *Low impact living: A field guide to ecological, affordable community building*, London: Routledge and Earthscan.

Clifford, J. (1997) *Routes: Travel and translation in the late twentieth century*, Cambridge, MA: Harvard University Press.

Clover, D. and Sandford, K. (eds) (2013) *Lifelong learning, the arts and community cultural engagement in the contemporary university*, Manchester: Manchester University Press.

Cockburn, C. (1998) *The space between us: Negotiating gender and national identities*, London: Zed.

Cockburn, C. (2012) *Anti-militarism: Political and gender dynamics of peace movements*, Basingstoke: Palgrave Macmillan.

Cohen, R. (1997) *Global diasporas: An introduction*, London: Routledge.

Cohen, R. (2006) *Migration and its enemies: Global capital, migrant labour, and the nation-state*, Aldershot: Ashgate.

Commission on Integration and Cohesion (2007) *Our shared future*, Wetherby: Department for Local Government and Communities.

Cowley, J. (1979) *Housing for people or for profit?*, London: Stage One.

Cowling, E. (2016) 'Alex Danchev: Historian whose wide-ranging work explored the power of art to change society', *The Guardian*, 30 September.

Craig, G. (2008) 'Community work and the state', in G. Craig, K. Popple and M. Shaw (eds) *Community development in theory and practice*, Nottingham: Spokesman, pp 176-94.

Craig, G. (2016) 'Community development in the UK: Whatever happened to class? A historical analysis', in M. Shaw and M. Mayo (eds) *Class, inequality and community development*, Bristol: Policy Press, pp 39-55.

Craig, G., Popple, K. and Shaw, M. (eds) (2008) *Community development in theory and practice*, Nottingham: Spokesman.

Craig, G., Mayo, M., Popple, K., Shaw, M. and Taylor, M. (eds) (2011) *The community development reader*, Bristol: Policy Press.

Dalrymple, W. (2002) *White Mughals: Love and betrayal in 18th-century India*, London: HarperCollins.

Dasgupta, S. and Lal, M. (2007) *The Indian family in transition: Reading literary and cultural texts*, London: Sage Publications.

Davis, M. (2007) *Planet of slums*, London: Verso.

Day, S. (2007) *On the game: Women in sex work*, London: Pluto.

Deakin, N. (1993) 'Privatism and partnership in urban policy', in C. Jones (ed) *New perspectives on the welfare state in Europe*, London: Routledge, pp 84-107.

Della Porta, D and Rucht, D. (2013) *Meeting democracy: Power and deliberation in global justice movements*, Cambridge: Cambridge University Press.

Dent, G., Gavron, K. and Young, M. (2006) *The new East End: Kinship, race and conflict*, London: Profile Books.

Dhaliwal, S. and Yuval-Davis, N. (eds) (2014) *Women against fundamentalism: Stories of dissent and solidarity*, London: Lawrence & Wishart.

Dickens, C. (1848 [2012]) *Dombey and son*, London: Penguin.

Dinham, A. (2009) *Faiths, public policy and civil society: Problems, policies, controversies*, Basingstoke: Palgrave Macmillan.

Dinham, A., Furbey, R. and Lowndes, V. (eds) (2009) *Faith in the public realm: Controversies, policies and practices*, Bristol: Policy Press.

Durkheim, E. (1952) *Suicide: A study in sociology*, London: Routledge & Kegan Paul [originally published in 1897].

Durrett, C. (2009) *The senior cohousing handbook*, Gabriola Island, Canada: New Society Publishers.

Dutta, A. (2007) *Development-induced displacement and human rights*, New Delhi, India: Deep and Deep.

Elliott, L. and Osborne, H. (2016) 'In 2025, only the rich will own their homes', *The Guardian,* 13 February, p 5.

Elson, D. and Pearson, R. (1981) 'Nimble fingers make cheap workers: An analysis of women's employment in the third world', *Feminist Review*, 7.

English, L. and Irving, C. (eds) (2015) *Feminism in community: Adult education for transformation,* Rotterdam, The Netherlands: Sense.

Esping-Andersen, G. (1985) *Politics against markets: The social democratic road to power*, Princeton, NJ: Princeton University Press.

Esping-Andersen, G. (1990) *The three worlds of welfare capitalism*, Oxford: Blackwell Publishing.

Faist, T. (2006) 'Extension du domaine de la lute: International migration and security before and after 11 September 2011', in A. Messina and G. Lahar (eds) *The migration reader*, London and Boulder, CO: Rienner, pp 609-15.

Farnsworth, K. and Irving, Z. (eds) (2015) *Social policy in times of austerity: Global economic crisis and the new politics of welfare*, Bristol: Policy Press.

Fekete, L. (2009) *A suitable enemy: Racism, migration and Islamophobia in Europe*, London: Pluto.

Fekete, L. (2014) 'Anti-fascism or anti-extremism?', *Race and Class*, vol 55, no 4, pp 29-39.

Ferrante, E. (2012) *My brilliant friend*, New York: Europa.

Finney, N. and Simpson, L. (2009) *'Sleepwalking to segregation'? Challenging myths about race and migration*, Bristol: Policy Press.

Fisher, R. (1994) *Let the people decide: Neighborhood organizing in America*, New York: Twayne.

Fisher, R. and Dimberg, K. (2016) 'The community organisers programme in England', *Journal of Community Practice*, vol 24, no 1, pp 94-108.

Foley, G. (1999) *Learning in social action: A contribution to understanding informal education,* London: Zed.

Foot, M. (1973) *Aneurin Bevan*, London: Davis: Poynter.

Foster, D. (2016) 'Eviction is the last refuge for poor tenants', *The Guardian,* 18 February.

Foster-Carter, A. (1989) 'The sociology of development', in M. Haralambos (ed) *Sociology: New directions*, Ormskirk: Causeway Press, pp 91-213.

Foucault, M. (1991) *Discipline and punish: The birth of the prison*, London: Penguin.

Fox Piven, F. and Minnite, L. (2015) 'Crisis, convulsion and the welfare state', in K. Farnsworth and Z. Irving (eds) *Social policy in times of austerity*, Bristol: Policy Press, pp 143-70.

Frank, A.G. (1969) *Capitalism and underdevelopment in Latin America*, New York: Monthly Review Press.

Freire, P. (1972) *Pedagogy of the oppressed*, Harmondsworth: Penguin.

Gallacher. W. (1978) *Revolt of the Clyde*, London: Lawrence & Wishart.

Gaventa, J. (2006) 'Finding the spaces for change: A power analysis', *Institute of Development Studies Bulletin*, vol 37, no 6, November, University of Sussex.

Gaventa, J. and Mayo, M. (2010) 'Spanning citizenship spaces through transnational coalitions: The Global Campaign for Education', in J. Gaventa and R. Tandon (eds) *Globalizing citizens: New dynamics of inclusion and exclusion*, London: Zed, pp 140-62.

Gaventa, J. and Tandon, R. (eds) (2010) *Globalizing citizens: New dynamics of inclusion and exclusion*, London: Zed.

GCE (Global Campaign for Education) (2007) *Education rights: A guide for practitioners and activists*, London: GCE.

Giddens, A. (1989) *Sociology*, Cambridge: Polity Press.

Gilroy, P. (1987) *There ain't no Black in the Union Jack: The cultural politics of race and nation*, London: Unwin Hyman.

Gilroy, P. (1993) *The Black Atlantic: Modernity and double consciousness*, Boston, MA: Harvard University Press.

Glick Schiller, N. and Faist, T. (eds) (2010) *Migration, development and transnationalism: A critical stance*, Oxford and New York: Berghan Books.

Glyn, S. (2012) 'Regeneration in interesting times: A story of privatisation and gentrification in a peripheral Scottish city', in G. Bridges, T. Butler and L. Lees (eds) *Mixed communities: Gentrification by stealth?*, Bristol: Policy Press, pp 185-207.

Gordimer, N. (2012) *No time like the present*, London: Bloomsbury.

Gramsci, A. (1986) *The modern prince and other writings*, New York: International Publishers.

Gray, J. (2015) *The soul of the marionette: A short enquiry into human freedom*, London: Allen Lane.

Hall, S. (1991) 'Old and new identities, old and new ethnicities', in A. King (ed) *Culture, globalization and the world system*, Basingstoke: Macmillan, pp 41-68.

Harvey, D. (1989) *The urban experience*, Oxford: Blackwell.

Harvey, D. (1990) *A brief history of neoliberalism*, New York and Oxford: Oxford University Press.

Harvey, D. (2008) *Limits to capital,* London: Verso.

Harvey, D. (2010) *The enigma of capital*, Cambridge: Polity Press.

Harvey, H. (2013) *Rebel cities: From the right to the city to the urban revolution*, London: Verso.

Hassan, M.A. (2013) 'Transnational active citizens: Theorizing the experiences of young Somali males in London', Unpublished PhD thesis, Goldsmiths, University of London.

Hewitt, R. (2005) *White backlash and the politics of multiculturalism*, Cambridge: Cambridge University Press.

Hickman, M., Mai, N. and Crowley, H. (2012) *Migration and social cohesion in the UK*, Basingstoke: Palgrave Macmillan.

Hills, J. (2015) *Good times, bad times: The welfare myth of them and us*, Bristol: Policy Press.

Hoggett, P. (2000) *Emotional life and the politics of welfare*, Basingstoke: Palgrave Macmillan.

Hoggett, P., Wilkinson, H. and Beedell, P. (2013) 'Fairness and the politics of resentment', *Journal of Social Policy*, vol 42, no 3, pp 567-85.

Holgate, J. (2009) 'London citizens and the campaign for a living wage', in J. McBride and I. Greenwood (eds) *Community unions: A comparative analysis of concepts and contexts*, Basingstoke: Palgrave Macmillan, pp 49-74.

Holgate, J. (2015) *Community organising and the implications for union revitalisation*, ETUI Policy Brief, Brussels: European Trade Union Institute (http://etui.org/content/download/20154/165291/file/Policy+Brief+2015.04+Holgate.pdf).

Holton, R. (2008) *Global networks*, Basingstoke: Palgrave Macmillan.

Horst, C. (2006) *Transnational nomads: How Somalis cope with refugee life in the Dadaab camp of Kenya*, Oxford: Berghan.

Hoque, A. (2015) *British-Islamic identity: Third-generation Bangladeshis from East London*, London: Trentham Books.

Hudson, M., Philips, J., Ray, K. and Barnes, H. (2007) *Social cohesion in diverse communities*, York: Joseph Rowntree Foundation.

Jackson, K. (1995) 'Popular education and the state: A new look at the community debate', in M. Mayo and J. Thompson (eds) *Adult learning, critical intelligence and social change*, Leicester: NIACE, pp 182-203.

Jewison, N. and Macgregor, S. (1997) *Transforming cities: New spatial divisions and social transformation,* London: Routledge.

Jones, H. (2013) *Negotiating cohesion, inequality and change*, Bristol: Policy Press.

Jones, H., Jones, V. and Cock, J.C. (2013) 'Impact measurement or agenda-setting', in M. Mayo, Z. Mendiwelso-Bendek and C. Pateman (eds) *Community research for community development*, Basingstoke: Palgrave Macmillan, pp 43-64.

Jones, O. (2011) *Chavs: The demonization of the working class*, London: Verso.

Kalra, V., Kaur, R. and Hutnyk, J. (2005) *Diaspora and hybridity*, London: Sage.

Kane, L. (2001) *Popular education and social change in Latin America*, London: Latin America Bureau.

Kapitan, T. (1995) 'Free will problem', in R. Audi (ed) *Cambridge dictionary of philosophy*, Cambridge: Cambridge University Press, pp 280-2.

Kenny, K. (2013) *Diaspora: A very short introduction*, Oxford: Oxford University Press.

Kenny, S., Taylor, M., Onyx, J. and Mayo, M. (2015) *Challenging the third sector: Global prospects for active citizenship*, Bristol: Policy Press.

Kill the Housing Bill (2015) info@defendcouncilhousing.org.uk

Kleist, N. (2010) 'Negotiating respectable masculinity: Gender and recognition in the Somali diaspora', *African Diaspora*, vol 3, pp 185-206.

Knowles, C. and Harper, D. (2009) *Hong Kong: Migrant lives, landscapes and journeys*, Chicago, IL: Chicago University Press.

Koessl, G. and Mayo, M. (2015) *Reversing the loss of social housing via estate regeneration in London*, London: Unite the Union.

Koh, H.H. (2006) 'The new global slave trade', in K. Tunstall (ed) *Displacement, asylum, migration*, Oxford: Oxford University Press, pp 232-63.

Kundnani, A. (2012) 'Radicalisation; the journey of a concept', *Race and Class*, vol 54, no 2, pp 3-25.

Kundnani, A. (2014) *The Muslims are coming! Islamophobia, extremism and the domestic war on terror*, London: Verso.

Kwei, S. (2014) 'Focus E15 Mums have fought for the right to a home. This is only the start', *The Guardian*, 5 October (www.theguardian. com/commentisfree/2014/oct/05/focus-e15-mums-fight-for-right-to-home).

Lapavitsas, C. (2013) *Profiting without producing: How finance exploits us all*, London: Verso.

Ledwith, M. (2005) *Community development: A critical approach*, Bristol: Policy Press.

Lewis, H., Dwyer, P., Hodkinson, S. and Waite, L. (2015) *Precarious lives: Forced labour, exploitation and asylum*, Bristol: Policy Press.

Ley, D. (2012) 'Social mixing and the historical geography of gentrification', in G. Bridges, T. Butler and L. Lees (eds) *Mixed communities: Gentrification by stealth?*, Bristol: Policy Press, pp 53-68.

LGA (Local Government Association) (2002) *Guidance on community cohesion*, London: LGA (www.tedcantle.co.uk/publications/006%20 Guidance%20on%20Community%20Cohesion%20LGA%202002. pdf).

Lindblom, C.E. (1977) *Politics and markets: The world's political-economic systems*, New York: Basic Books.

Lindley, A. (2010) *The early morning call*, Oxford: Berghan.

London Assembly Housing Committee (2015) *Knock it down or do it up?*, London: London Assembly Housing Committee.

Lukes, S. (2004) *Power: A radical view*, Basingstoke: Palgrave Macmillan.

MacColl, E. and Seeger, P. (1963) *Songbook*, New York and London: Oak and Music Sales.

McGhee, D. (2008) *The end of multiculturalism? Terrorism, integration and human rights*, Maidenhead: Open University Press.

McKenzie, L. (2015) *Getting by: Estates, class and culture in austerity Britain*, Bristol: Policy Press.

McVeigh, T. (2015) 'London clinic is a lifeline for the refugees afraid to use the NHS', *The Observer*, 27 December (www.theguardian.com/society/2015/dec/27/doctors-of-the-world-guardian-observer-charity-appeal-2015).

Marfleet, P. (2006) *Refugees in a global era*, Basingstoke: Palgrave Macmillan.

Martin, I. (1999) 'Introductory essay: Popular education and social movements in Scotland today' in J. Crowther, I. Martin and M. Shaw (eds) *Popular education and social movements in Scotland today*, Leicester: NIACE, pp 1-25.

Martinez-Torres, M. and Firmiano, F. (2016) 'Rural-urban alliances for community development through land reform from below', in M. Shaw and M. Mayo (eds) *Class, inequality and community development*, Bristol: Policy Press, pp 153-67.

Marx, K. (1968) *Marx and Engels, Selected works*, London: Lawrence & Wishart.

Massey, D. (1994) 'Double articulation: A place in the world', in A. Banner (ed) *Displacements,* Bloomington, IN: Indiana University Press, pp 110-21.

Massey, D. (2007) *World city*, Cambridge: Polity Press.

Massey, D., Arango, J., Hugo, G., Kouaouci, A., Pellegrino, A. and Taylor, J. (.2009) *Worlds in motion: Understanding international migration at the end of millennium*, Oxford: Oxford University Press

Matthews, P. and O'Brien, D. (2016) 'Connecting community to the post-regeneration era', in D. O'Brien and P. Matthews (eds) *After urban regeneration: Communities, policy and place*, Bristol: Policy Press, pp 27-43.

Mayo, M. (2008) 'Introduction: Community development, contestations, continuities and change', in G. Craig, K. Popple and M. Shaw (eds) *Community development in theory and practice*, Nottingham: Spokesman, pp 13-27.

Mayo, M. and Koessl, G. (2015) *Magna Carta today?*, London: Unite the Union.

Mayo, M. and Newman, I. (2014) *Tackling the housing crisis: Alternatives to declining standards, displacement and dispossession*, London: Centre for Labour and Social Studies.

Mayo, M. and Rooke, A. (2012) *AMICALL: Final evaluation report*, London: Centre for Urban and Community Research, Goldsmiths, University of London.

Mayo, M., Mediwelso-Bendek, Z. and Packham, C. (eds) (2013) *Community research for community development*, Basingstoke: Palgrave Macmillan.

Mayo, M., Tucker, P. with Danaher, M. (2016) 'Community unionism: looking backwards, looking forwards', in M. Shaw and M. Mayo (eds) *Class, inequality and community development*, Bristol: Policy Press, pp 235–50.

Mayo, M., Koessl, G., Scott, M. and Slater, I. (2014) *Access to justice in disadvantaged communities*, Bristol: Policy Press.

Meiksins Wood, E. (1991) *The pristine culture of capitalism: A historical essay on old regimes and modern states*, London: Verso.

Mercer, C., Page, B. and Evans, M. (2008) *Development and the African diaspora: Place and the politics of home*, London: Zed.

Meyers, J. (2012) 'Thomas Mann in America', *Michigan Quarterly Review*, vol 51, issue 4 (http://hdl.handle.net/2027/spo.act2080.0051.419).

Milbourne, L. (2013) *Voluntary sector in transition: Hard times or new opportunities?*, Bristol: Policy Press.

Mills, C. Wright (1959) *The sociological imagination*, Oxford: Oxford University Press.

Milton, N. (1973) *John Maclean*, London: Pluto Press.

Mitter, S. (1986) *Common fate, common bond: Women in the global economy*, London: Pluto.

Mohammadi, K. (2011) *The cypress tree: A love letter to Iran*, London: Bloomsbury.

Moore, B. (1966) *Social origins of dictatorship and democracy: Lord and peasant in the making of the modern world*, Harmondsworth: Penguin.

Newbury, D. (2013) *People apart: 1950s Cape Town revisited: Photographs by Bryan Heseltine*, London: Black Dog.

Newell, P. and Wheeler, J. (2006) *Rights, resources and the politics of accountability*, London: Zed.

Newell, P. with Anand, V., Arjjumend, H., Kumar, S. and Ranga Rao, A. (2006) 'Corporate accountability and citizen action', in P. Newell and J. Wheeler (eds) *Rights, resources and the politics of accountability*, London: Zed, pp 166–85.

Ngugi wa Thiong'o (2015) 'Despite decades of exile, I still feel the pull of my homeland', *The Guardian*, 9 September (www.theguardian.com/commentisfree/2015/sep/09/exile-kenya-home-moi-dictatorship).

Nussbaum, M.C. (2003) 'Capabilities as fundamental entitlements: Sen and social justice', *Feminist Economics*, vol 9, no 2-3, pp 33-59.

Nussbaum, M.C. (2007) *The clash within: Democracy, religious violence and India's future*, Cambridge, MA: Harvard University Press.

O'Connell Davidson, J. (2015) *Modern slavery: The margins of freedom*, Basingstoke: Palgrave Macmillan.

O'Malley, J. (1977) *The politics of community action*, London: Pluto.

Osbourne, L. (2014) *The forgiven*, London: Vintage Books.

Pegg, D. (2016) 'Thousands of homes left empty in London', *The Guardian,* 22 February.

Popple, K. (2006) 'The first forty years of the CDJ', *Community Development Journal*, vol 43, no 1, pp 1-18.

Popple, K. (2015) *Analysing community work*, Maidenhead: Open University Press.

Poulantzas, N. (1972) 'The problem of the capitalist state', in R. Blackburn (ed) *Social science readings in critical theory*, New York: Pantheon Books, pp 238-62.

Prebble, J. (1963) *The Highland Clearances*, Harmondsworth: Penguin.

Raina, V., Chowdhury, A. and Chowdhury, S. (1997) *The dispossessed – Victims of development in Asia*, Hong Kong: ARENA.

Ratcliffe, P. (2004) *Race, ethnicity and difference: Imagining the inclusive society*, Maidenhead: Open University Press.

Ratcliffe, P. and Newman, I. (eds) (2011) *Promoting social cohesion: Implications for policy and evaluation*, Bristol: Policy Press.

Report of the Commission on Religion and Belief in British Public Life (2015) *Living with difference: Community, diversity and the common good*, Cambridge: The Woolf Institute (https://corablivingwithdifference. files.wordpress.com/2015/12/living-with-difference-online.pdf).

Robson, T. (2000) *The state and community action*, London: Pluto.

Rooke, A. (2013) 'Contradiction, collaboration and criticality: Researching empowerment and citizenship in community-based art', in M. Mayo, Z. Mendiwelso-Bendek and C. Packham (eds) *Community research for community development*, Basingstoke: Palgrave Macmillan, pp 150-69.

Rose, J. (2006) 'Displacement in Zion', in K. Tunstall (ed) *Displacement, asylum and migrants*, Oxford: Oxford University Press, pp 264-90.

Rosengarten, L. (2015) *Survival and conscience: From the shadows of Nazi Germany to the Jewish boat to Gaza*, Charlottesville, VA: Just World Books.

Roy, A. (1999) *The cost of living*, London: Flamingo.

Sandel, M. (1998) *Liberalism and the limits of justice* (2nd edn), Cambridge: Cambridge University Press.

Sanders, T. (2016) 'Concluding thoughts: The consequences of a "not-so-big society"', in M. Harrison and T. Sanders (eds) *Social policies and social control*, Bristol: Policy Press, pp 199-201.

Sassen, S. (2007) *A sociology of globalization*, New York and London: W.W. Norton.

Sassen, S. (2014) *Expulsions: Brutality and complexity in the global economy*, Cambridge, MA: Belknap, Harvard University Press.

Scholte, J.A. (2005) *Globalization: A critical introduction* (2nd edn), Basingstoke: Palgrave Macmillan.

Scott, P. (1984) *The Raj quartet*, New York: William Morrow & Co.

Scott, P. (1997) *Staying on*, London: Heinemann.

Sebald, W.G. (1997) *The emigrants*, London: Harvill Press.

Sen, A. (1992) *Inequality reexamined*, Oxford: Oxford University Press.

Sen, A. (2006) *Identity and violence*, London: Penguin Books.

Sennett, R. (1976) *The fall of the public man*, New York and London: W.W. Norton.

Shaw, M. and Martin, I. (2008) 'Community work, citizenship and democracy: Remaking the connections', in G. Craig, K. Popple and M. Shaw (eds) *Community development in theory and practice*, Nottingham: Spokesman, pp 296-308.

Slovo, G. (2016) '1960s: "Becoming a refugee is not a choice"', *The Guardian*, 28 July.

Spencer, S., Ruhs, M., Anderson, B. and Rogaly, B. (2007) *Migrants' lives beyond the workplace: The experiences of Central and Eastern Europeans in the UK*, York: Joseph Rowntree Foundation.

Stacey, M. (1969) 'The myth of community studies', *British Journal of Sociology*, vol 20, no 2, pp 134-47.

Steinbeck, J. (1990) *The grapes of wrath*, London: Minerva [originally published in 1939].

Sukarieh, M. and Tannock, S. (2015) 'The deradicalisation of education: Terror, youth and the assault on learning', *Race and Class*, vol 57, no 2, pp 22-38.

Sullivan, M. (2009) 'Somalis plot suicide blitz on UK target', *The Sun*, 5 August, quoted in Hassan, M.A. (2013) 'Transnational active citizens: Theorizing the experiences of young Somali males in London', Unpublished PhD thesis, Goldsmiths, University of London.

Taylor, M. and Wilson, M. (2016) 'Community organising for social change: The scope for class politics', in M. Shaw and M. Mayo (eds) *Class, inequality and community development*, Bristol: Policy Press, pp 219-34.

Thukral, E.G. (ed) (1992) *Big dams, displaced people: Rivers of sorrow, rivers of change*, New Delhi and London: Sage Publications.

Tiller, C. (2013) 'Participatory arts and community development', in M. Mayo, Z. Mendiwelso-Bendek and C. Packham (eds) *Community research for community development*, Basingstoke: Palgrave Macmillan, pp 133-49.

Toibin, C. (2009) *Brooklyn*, London: Penguin Books, Random House.

Tunstall, K. (2006) (ed) *Displacement, asylum, migration: The Oxford Amnesty lectures 2004*, Oxford: Oxford University Press.

Tyler, I. (2013) *Revolting subjects: Social abjection and resistance in neoliberal Britain*, London: Zed.

Umunna, C. (2016) 'There is a way to merge our parallel lives', *The Guardian*, 24 May 2016.

UNHCR (United Nations Refugee Agency) (2015) '"Refugee" or "migrant" – Which is right?', UNHCR Viewpoint, 27 August (www.unhcr.ie/news/irish-story/unhcr-viewpoint-refugee-or-migrant-which-is-right).

Valman, N. (2016) 'Pepper to throw at fascists: The forgotten women of Cable Street', *New Statesman*, 4 October (www.newstatesman.com/politics/feminism/2016/10/pepper-throw-fascists-forgotten-women-cable-street).

Vergara-Camus, L. (2014) *Land and freedom: The MST, the Zapatistas and peasant alternatives*, London: Verso.

Verkaik, R. (2009) 'How MI5 blackmails British Muslims', *The Independent*, 21 May.

Vertovec, S. (2009) *Transnationalism*, London: Routledge.

Wallerstein, I. (1974) *The modern world-system 1: Capitalist agriculture and the origins of the European world-economy in the sixteenth century*, New York: Academic Press.

Waltham Forest Socialist Party (2016) *Butterfields didn't budge: How tenants on one East London estate saved their homes*, London: Waltham Forest Socialist Party.

Watt, D. and Jones, A. (2015) *Catching hell and doing well: Black women in the UK*, London: Trentham.

Weeks, J. (2014) *Economics of the 1%*, London: Anthem.

Wei, S. and Ashworth, L. (2016) 'Academics speak out against Prevent strategy', *Varsity*, 11 May (www.varsity.co.uk/news/10238).

Wilks-Heeg, S. (2016) 'Urban policy and communities', in D. O'Brien and P. Matthews (eds) *After urban regeneration: Communities, policies and place*, Bristol: Policy Press, pp 9-25.

Williams, F. (1989) *Social policy: A critical introduction*, Cambridge: Polity Press.

Williams, F. (2010) 'Migration and care: Theories, concepts and challenges', *Social Policy and Society*, vol 9, no 3, pp 385-96.

Williams, R. (1976) *Keywords: A vocabulary of culture and society*, London: Fontana Paperbacks.

Williams, R. (1988) *Keywords: A vocabulary of culture and society* (2nd edn), London: Fontana Paperbacks.

Willmott, P. and Young, M. (1971) *Family and kinship in a London suburb*, London: Routledge & Kegan Paul.

Wills, J. (2016) *Locating localism: Statecraft, citizenship and democracy*, Bristol: Policy Press.

Young, M. and Willmott, P. (1957) *Family and Kinship in East London*, London: Routledge and Kegan Paul

Young, M. and Willmott, P. (2007) *Family and kinship in East London*, Harmondsworth: Penguin [with new Introduction].

Zweig, S. (2011) *Beware of pity*, London: Pushkin Press.

Index